# Corporate Governance

## A Practical Guide to the Legal Frameworks and International Codes of Practice

Alan Calder

KOGAN
PAGE

London and Philadelphia

**Publisher's note**

Every possible effort has been made to ensure that the information contained in this book is accurate at the time of going to press, and the publishers and author cannot accept responsibility for any errors or omissions, however caused. No responsibility for loss or damage occasioned to any person acting, or refraining from action, as a result of the material in this publication can be accepted by the editor, the publisher or the author.

First published in Great Britain and the United States in 2008 by Kogan Page Limited
Reprinted 2008

120 Pentonville Road
London  N1 9JN
United Kingdom
www.koganpage.com

525 South 4th Street, #241
Philadelphia  PA 19147
USA

© Alan Calder, 2008

ISBN  978 0 7494 4817 2

**British Library Cataloguing-in-Publication Data**

A CIP record for this book is available from the British Library.

**Library of Congress Cataloging-in-Publication Data**

Calder, Alan, 1957–
    Corporate governance : a practical guide to the legal frameworks and
international codes of practice / Alan Calder.
        p. cm.
    Includes bibliographical references and index.
    ISBN 978-0-7494-4817-2
  1. Corporate governance––Law and legislation. 2. International business
enterprises––Law and legislation. 3. Corporate governance––Law and legislation––
Great Britain. I. Title.
    K1327.C35 2008
    346'.0664––dc22

                                        2007043995

Typeset by JS Typesetting Ltd, Porthcawl, Mid Glamorgan
Printed and bound in Great Britain by Biddles Ltd, King's Lynn, Norfolk

# Contents

# Introduction

In the 21st century, corporate governance has become critical for all medium and large organizations. Those without a governance strategy face significant risks; those with one perform measurably better. But what is corporate governance, and what do directors of companies – both quoted and unquoted – need to know? This book aims to provide a clear description for managers and executives that will enable them to identify the practical steps necessary to meet today's corporate governance requirements.

Corporations work within a governance framework which is set first by the law and then by regulations emanating from the regulatory bodies to which they are subject. In addition, publicly quoted companies are subject to their shareholders in general meeting and all companies to the forces of public opinion.[1]

## BACKGROUND

The 'greed is good' business philosophy of the 1980s and 1990s seemed to give way at the end of the 20th century to a 'looting is good' approach. Catastrophic financial failure is, of course, a characteristic of the business cycle and it is not uncommon for a downturn in the cycle to expose organizations that have been playing fast and loose with their shareholders' funds. Looting has happened before: BCCI and Maxwell Communications are good examples. Corporate collapse, originating in a failure of internal control, has happened before: Barings Bank is an instance.

The spate of collapses and financial failures at the end of the internet bubble, though, suggested a systemic weakness, and one whose increasingly worldwide implications had a significant, negative knock-on effect on already problematic pension funds and pensioner assets. Enron, WorldCom, Marconi, Parmalat and many other corporate disasters are the storm damage of unbridled executive authority. Shareholders are not enthusiastic about continued losses on this scale.

Governments, already grappling with the challenge of funding the pensions of an inexorably greying population bulge, cannot afford further wanton asset destruction and have started applying themselves to rooting out corporate misbehaviour. They are doing this through a combination of overt regulatory action and slightly more covert pressure on institutional investors to stand up for their rights as shareholders and to more determinedly exercise their de facto responsibility to insist on proper governance from those organizations in which they are invested.

The concept of governance is a simple one: it 'is the system by which business corporations are directed and controlled'.[2] The 'holy trinity' of good corporate governance has long been seen as shareholder rights, transparency and board accountability.

# GOVERNANCE

While corporate governance appears overtly concerned with board structure, executive compensation and shareholder reporting, the underlying assumption is that the *board* is responsible for managing the business and controlling the risks to the organization's assets and trading future. Across the OECD,[3] institutions, investors, regulatory bodies and governments are converging[4] around a common understanding of corporate governance, and in the developing world, corporate governance is increasingly seen as a basic 'cost of entry' into the global capital markets.

There are still substantial practical differences between corporate governance frameworks in different jurisdictions. The US corporate governance framework has a far higher degree of compulsion about it than does the United Kingdom's 'comply or explain' regime, and most continental European and South Asian regimes are, comparatively, still in their infancy. Effective corporate governance is transparent, protects the rights of shareholders, includes both strategic and operational risk management, is as interested in long-term earning potential as it is in actual short-term earnings, holds directors accountable for their stewardship of the business, and ensures that directors exercise their fiduciary duties responsibly.

## Fiduciary duties

Corporate governance could be thought of as the combined statutory and non-statutory framework within which boards of directors exercise their fiduciary duties to the organizations that appoint them. The key issue is that 'directors owe to shareholders, or perhaps to the corporation, two basic fiduciary duties: the duty of loyalty and the duty of care'.[5]

The duty of care is very important, and the foundation perhaps for the others: the duty to pay attention and to try to make good decisions. The decisions do not actually have to be good ones; the directors are simply required to *try* to make good decisions. The United States, for instance, has the 'business judgement rule', also known as the 'doctrine of non-interference'. This allows directors to take business risks, even extreme ones, without fear of legal penalty for failure.

In the United Kingdom, the fiduciary duties of directors have now been given statutory strength: the Companies Act 2006 identifies seven specific directors' 'general' duties:[6]

1.  a duty to act within powers;

2.  a duty to promote the success of the company;

3.  a duty to exercise reasonable judgement;

4.  a duty to exercise reasonable care, skill and diligence;

5.  a duty to avoid conflicts of interest;

6.  a duty not to accept benefits from third parties;

7.  a duty to declare an interest in proposed transactions or arrangements.

An eighth duty might be added to these, although it ought to be taken as read: to obey the law and ensure that the company does so, too. Ongoing misdemeanours by companies suggest that this basic requirement may not be that well understood!

## Governance frameworks

The cost of corporate failure is, in any case, borne by shareholders, by employees, by suppliers and by other stakeholders in the organization. The United Kingdom, in the Cadbury, Greenbury and Turnbull reports of the late 1990s, led the way for the OECD in defining how the directors' duty of care – in respect of executive compensation and board management – should be exercised.

Progress, particularly in the aftermath of the post-Internet Bubble scandals, has continued. The UK's revised Combined Code is now explicit in saying that all directors are required to 'provide entrepreneurial leadership of the company within a framework of prudent and effective controls which enable *risk to be assessed and managed.*'[7] This recognizes the need for a risk management framework and leaves little room for imprudent risk-taking. Directors' duties in the UK have now been enshrined in statute.

The US Sarbanes–Oxley Act of 2002 (SOX) required a radical improvement in US corporate governance practices and has cast a long shadow across a world that has business dealings with US listed companies. SOX mandated the adoption, by US listed companies, of an appropriate system of internal control and, in parallel, required directors to start monitoring and reporting operational risk. SOX and the associated audit regime have attracted real interest from within the European Union (EU), whose evolving law is significantly influenced by the experience of SOX.

Similar governance requirements have emerged elsewhere in the OECD, and the OECD Principles of Corporate Governance, first published in 1999, were revised in 2004.

The spread of the International Financial Reporting Standards (IFRS) across the EU has contributed to a significant convergence in financial reporting and requirements in respect of internal controls. The ongoing convergence of IFRS and US Generally Accepted Accounting Principles (GAAP) will drive convergence between auditing, risk management and corporate governance expectations and practices.

Australia, South Africa and other countries outside the EU already have strong governance frameworks and are taking steps to further strengthen and improve them. Across South Asia and in a number of African and South American countries, the need for effective corporate governance regimes is also being increasingly recognized.

As the tendrils of the corporate governance movement spread out across the financial sphere and dig deeper into national and international corporate culture, so the pressure on directors to know and understand what is expected of them, and to position themselves for appropriate action, is growing.

## Requirements on directors

Corporate governance is a daily newspaper subject and, to some extent or another, company directors – and the directors of public sector and quasi-autonomous governmental organizations (known in the UK as 'quangos') – all want to know what it really means for them. What is good corporate governance practice? To whom does the Combined Code really apply? Is SOX important outside the United States? Should the directors of privately owned UK companies pay the same attention to corporate governance as those of FTSE 100 companies? What is the EU up to, and what difference will it make?

The vast majority of company directors are law-abiding business people. 'Corporate governance' can seem to them like unnecessary bureaucracy and red tape that interferes with the effective management of their company; this book is designed to provide all directors with clarity about what is – and what is not – good governance practice in their type of organization.

# NOTES

1. Sir Adrian Cadbury (1998) 'The future of governance: the rules of the game', *Journal of General Management*, **24** (1), Autumn.
2. OECD (1999) *OECD Principles of Corporate Governance*, OECD, Paris.
3. The Organization for Economic Cooperation and Development, an international agency that endeavours to do exactly what its title suggests.
4. See Alan Calder (2005) *IT Governance: Guidelines for directors*, IT Governance Publishing, Ely.
5. Professor Bernard S Black, Stanford Law School, Presentation at Third Asian Roundtable on Corporate Governance, April 2001.
6. Companies Act 2006, chapter 2, paras 170–77.
7. Financial Reporting Council (2003) *UK Revised Combined Code, Higgs Suggestions for Good Practice*, January, FRC, London.

# 1

# Corporate governance – the historical background

A corporation is 'a large company authorized to act as a single entity and recognized as such in law'.[1] This simple definition of the modern corporation identifies its two essential characteristics: it has a legal personality and it exists within a legal framework. The corporate personality and the legal framework have evolved over centuries, and have both statutory and non-statutory elements to them.

While it is not the purpose of this book to provide a detailed history of corporate governance,[2] it might be useful to have a brief survey of the background to the emergence of a multifaceted discipline that today seems to pervade more levels of business activity than strictly necessary.

## PRE-MODERN TIMES

What is today called entrepreneurialism was, for much of the Middle Ages (by which I mean the period following the collapse the Roman Empire in the West through until the Enlightenment), practised more obviously by baronial marauders and the Church than by commercially astute private business people. Such people did exist: the commercial and trading activity of the world was their creation. Generally, however, their capital was their own and was limited to what they or their families had managed to generate, and their business successes were highly dependent on their own close personal supervision. Their wealth – and their person – was, for centuries, at the mercy of avaricious nobles, royals or the Church. It was also at the mercy of rivals, and of nature: if a risk went against you, you could lose everything that you had earned.

The emergence during this period of a body of canon law that recognized the Church as a body separate from its members,[3] which was greater than and could outlive any individual member, enabled the Church to develop a vast wealth and was an essential precursor to today's corporation.

Corporations, or companies, began to emerge under charters granted by monarchs or governments to undertake operations that were potentially risky and/or highly expensive, which individuals were therefore unlikely to undertake on their own – particularly if there might be no limit to their potential losses if the venture were to fail.

# EMERGENCE OF THE PRE-MODERN CORPORATION

The Dutch East India Company, created in 1601 by charter from the States-General of the Netherlands, was granted a 21-year monopoly to exploit Asia. The company (known acronymically as the VOC) issued stock to the business chambers in the main port cities of the Netherlands and, through them, many smaller investors as well. This was a significant improvement on the earlier corporate model, which saw investors set up companies for the duration of a single voyage and then liquidate them on return. Monopolization reduced competition, of course; it also led to the appointment of a governor-general to control the company's business, and the creation of a Council of the Indies to control the governor-general.

This model was very successful, and the VOC survived for some 200 years, paying a substantial annual dividend throughout the period. It also ushered in a period of corporate colonialism, in which joint stock companies such as the Hudson Bay Company, the East India Company and so on gave many other nations their own experience – both good and bad – of such companies' effectiveness.

The creation of joint stock companies was then, for a period of about 100 years, restricted by the British government in order to limit competition in a number of sectors.[4]

The modern corporation emerged from this background. The dramatic economic, trading and financial expansion of the early 18th century and similarly world-changing industrialization and development of the mid-19th century made this protectionist approach untenable. Many businesses operated as unincorporated associations, without their own independent legal personalities, and this made litigation – amongst other things – complex and difficult. The oscillation between what we prefer to describe as the business cycle and what is, sometimes in reality, actually the 'boom and bust' cycle led entrepreneurs to invent other forms of company, including what were called Deed of Settlement companies. The UK finally liberated the corporation, passing the world's first Companies Act, the Joint Stock Companies Act of 1844.

Corporations continued, in practice and in law, to provide entrepreneurs and their financial backers with no method of limiting their losses if a risky venture failed. Corporate bankruptcy could lead to personal bankruptcy until, in the UK, shareholders' liabilities were formally limited with the Limited Liability Act of 1855.

The United States, in the meantime, had been creating industrial corporations since 1813[5] and had allowed them to grow, and quite quickly they came to outperform those of the UK and Europe. They've continued growing and continued inventing and perfecting new methods for creating wealth.

And that's where the problem lies.

# THE MODERN CORPORATION

The modern corporation has four significant legal characteristics:

1.  It is a legal entity, with a 'personality' separate from that of its members. It can therefore:

    a.   make arrangements to govern its own activities;

    b.   sue and be sued;

    c.   purchase, hold and dispose of assets in its own name;

    d.   hire staff, agents and contractors;

    e.   enter into commercial contracts in its own name.

2.  It has transferable shares, which (subject at times to shareholder agreements) enable shareholders to transfer part or all of their ownership of the corporation without affecting its existence.

3.  It has independence from its shareholders, so that the corporation's survival is not dependent on the continuing life of those shareholders.

4.  It has limited liability, so that the shareholders have no direct liability in respect of the actions of the corporation, its debts, its contracts or the outcomes of its actions.

It is these characteristics that make the modern corporation a vehicle for the ongoing creation of wealth on an extreme scale while, at the same time, providing unscrupulous business managers and stock brokers with an easy and fast way to make themselves very substantial fortunes with a minimum of personal financial risk.

Stock market booms provide clear evidence that private citizens, as much as professional investors, are attracted by opportunities to make a quick return on an investment; the fact that you could buy a share in a modern corporation without becoming involved in managing it and without taking any risk greater than the cost of its purchase made investing an attractive option for many – particularly if the investment was growing and the shares could in due course be sold to someone else at a tidy profit.

Speculators created share booms; reality created the subsequent busts. Governments do not approve of boom and bust, as they usually have to pick up the pieces. Modern corporate law – and its regulatory framework – has evolved to protect members of the voting public both from their own greed and from unscrupulous fellow shareholders.

In the United States, for instance, in the early 1900s individual states passed what were known as 'Blue Sky' laws, to prohibit fraudsters selling shares in anything as ethereal as the sky. These laws were, however, insufficient to prevent the great boom of the 1920s or the subsequent Great Crash. The consequences of the Great Crash led the US Congress to create a single national securities regulator, the US Securities and Exchange Commission (the SEC), in 1933, followed, in 1934, by the Securities Exchange Act.

In the UK, what were known as the 'City Rules' provided the framework for how UK listed companies were governed. These rules were essentially self-regulatory in nature, and they relied on the fact that the City was contained in a square mile and that most of the key figures knew one another. Peer pressure was therefore an effective regulatory method, and the threat of expulsion from the 'club' was sufficient sanction to contain most excessive behaviours.

The links between individuals and an environment within which enlightened self-interest was an effective regulatory force broke down rapidly after the UK's 'Big Bang' in 1986, when the age-old barriers between different sorts of financial firms were removed and foreign (particularly US) financial houses were able to enter the City. US firms tended to work on the basis that whatever wasn't specifically forbidden by law was allowed, and they were more interested in generating wealth today than in developing and preserving corporate reputation for the long term.

The financial boom of the 1980s led, inevitably, to a bust. Cyclical peaks and troughs are always characterized by spectacular corporate failures, not all of which are caused entirely by the changing business environment: companies that had over-expanded, or whose claimed performance was much greater than the underlying one, could not survive the real downturn in demand. Scandals like Polly Peck, BCCI and the Maxwell Corporation had begun to suggest that there were weaknesses in the framework within which they operated.

# EMERGENCE OF THE 'CORPORATE GOVERNANCE' CONCEPT

It appears that some of the earliest work in the world on the subject of corporate governance was done by the UK's Institute of Chartered Secretaries and Administrators, which published a series of papers in 1979 on corporate governance, in which boardroom responsibilities were examined. The term 'Corporate Governance' first gained prominence when it was used in *The Independent Director* by Robert Tricker.[6] He described corporate governance, in *Corporate Governance* (1984), as being 'concerned with the way corporate entities are governed, as distinct from the way businesses within those companies are managed. Corporate Governance addresses the issues faced by boards of directors, such as the interaction with top management, and relationships with the owners and others interested in the affairs of the company'.[7]

# THEORIES OF CORPORATE GOVERNANCE

There are, essentially, three theories of corporate governance: the stewardship theory, the agency theory and the market theory.

The stewardship theory of corporate governance holds that, because people can be trusted to act in the public good in general and in the interests of their shareholders in particular, it makes sense to create management and authority structures that, because they provide unified command and facilitate autonomous decision making, enable companies to act (and react) quickly and decisively to market opportunities. This approach leads, for instance, to the combination of the roles of chair and CEO, and for audit committees to be either non-existent or lightweight. Resistance to the modern corporate governance movement today tends to be based on this theory.

The agency theory of corporate governance, on the other hand, sees shareholders as the principals and management as their agents. Agents will, however, act with rational self-interest: as employee directors of a company, they will tend to maximize their monetary compensation, job stability and other perks, and do no more than seek to appease shareholders. They cannot, in other words, be expected to act in the interests of the shareholders. They need, instead, to be monitored and controlled to ensure that the principals' best interests are served. This theory is the basis for most of today's corporate governance activity.

The market theory of corporate governance holds that it doesn't really matter whether managers see themselves as stewards or agents, because shareholders will simply sell in the market the stocks and shares of those companies whose directors are not generating adequate returns for their investment. To the extent that this theory was genuinely held, it was fatally undermined by the corporate scandals at the turn of the century: shareholders in Enron (including many of its employees) were unable to sell their shares (many of which were held in pension plans) once it became clear that the company's governance was wholly inadequate.

# THE CADBURY REPORT

The UK's financial and corporate activity is, as I said earlier, highly centralized in the City of London. The City's roots in self-regulating medieval guilds continued into the modern era, and it developed a quasi-legal, self-regulatory approach to many aspects of corporate activity: key professions, such as lawyers and accountants, were self-regulated (by recognized professional bodies, or RPBs), as were the insurance market (Lloyd's of London), the pensions sector (the Pensions and Investment Authority), investment businesses (through their own self-regulatory organizations or SROs), the securities market (the Securities and Futures Association) and, of course, the London Stock Exchange itself.

This started changing in 1986, with the passage of the Financial Services Act, which was intended to increase investor protection and improve regulation of financial services. The United Kingdom's pension mis-selling scandal (the period between 29 April 1988 and 30 June 1994, during which individuals were encouraged to leave secure final-salary occupational pensions for apparently more attractive money-purchase personal pensions, which led to the (temporary) enrichment of pension sales forces) helped to fatally undermine belief in the self-regulating approach as being effective. The Financial Services and Markets Act

2000 brought about a more comprehensive shift to today's statutory framework of regulation.

The UK approach to corporate governance still is essentially self-regulatory in character and usually involves setting up a committee to deal with a specific issue.

The first committee of the modern corporate governance era was, however, set up in the United States. The Treadway Committee,[8] set up to investigate fraudulent financial reporting by Wall Street firms, preceded the Cadbury Committee, which was set up in May 1991 by the UK's Financial Reporting Council, the London Stock Exchange and the UK accountancy profession specifically to address the financial aspects of corporate governance.

The Cadbury Report (*The Financial Aspects of Corporate Governance*) was published on 1 December 1992.[9] 'The harsh economic climate… has exposed company reports and accounts to unusually close scrutiny. It is, however, the continuing concern about standards of financial reporting and accountability, heightened by BCCI, Maxwell and the controversy over directors' pay, which has kept corporate governance in the public eye.'[10] The committee's chairman, Sir Adrian Cadbury, described the setting for his committee's report and, in doing so, succinctly explained the role of corporate governance: 'The country's economy depends on the drive and efficiency of its companies. Thus the effectiveness with which their boards discharge their responsibilities determines Britain's competitive position. They must be free to drive their companies forward but exercise that freedom within a framework of effective accountability. This is the essence of any system of good corporate governance.'

The report's introduction provides a description of the role of corporate governance that is so lucid that it is still valid:

> Corporate Governance is the system by which companies are directed and controlled. Boards of directors are responsible for the governance of their companies. The shareholders' role in governance is to appoint the directors and the auditors and to satisfy themselves that an appropriate governance structure is in place. The responsibilities of the board include setting the company's strategic aims, providing the leadership to put them into effect, supervising the management of the business and reporting to shareholders on their stewardship. The board's actions are subject to laws, regulations and the shareholders in general meeting.

The Cadbury Committee's remit was specifically to address the financial aspects of corporate governance, 'the way in which boards set financial policy and oversee its implementation, including the use of financial controls, and the process whereby they report on the activities and progress of the company to the shareholders'. The Committee's report:

1.　reviewed the structure and responsibilities of boards of directors, and summarized its recommendations in a Code of Best Practice, which was aimed at boards of all listed companies in the UK ('but we would encourage as many other companies as possible to aim at meeting its requirements'):

    a.　there should be a balance of executive and non-executive directors on the board, so that no one group could dominate decision making, and non-executive directors should make up at least one-third of the board;

    b.　a majority of non-executive directors should be independent of management and free from any business or other relationship with the company and its management;

    c.　non-executive directors should be appointed for specific terms;

    d.　their service contracts should not exceed three years;

    e.　executive remuneration should be subject to a remuneration committee composed completely or largely of non-executive directors;

2.　reviewed the role of auditors, recommended the establishment of an audit committee consisting of at least three non-executives, and made a separate series of recommendations to the audit profession; and

3.　reviewed the rights and responsibilities of shareholders.

The Cadbury Report is recognized internationally as:

having been seminal in the development of corporate governance in the UK and elsewhere. It originated the self-regulation approach whereby reporting of compliance was part of the listing requirements for public companies. The emphasis on the board as a focal decision point could be said to be led by Cadbury, as could be the emphasis on appropriately constituted board sub-committees (remuneration, audit and nomination), independent non-executive directors and the separation of chairman and chief executive positions.[11]

A requirement was added to the London Stock Exchange's Listing Rules for companies to report whether or not they had followed the recommendations of each of the Cadbury Code's provisions and if not, to explain why not. It was further recommended that the company's auditors review this statement prior to release of the accounts.

This is the origin of what is now known as the 'comply or explain' approach to corporate governance.

# SARBANES–OXLEY

Although the OECD's first *Principles of Corporate Governance* (published in 1999, revised in 2004) were very much in the spirit of Cadbury, the United States went down a rather different route from that based on the UK's 'comply or explain' principle.

While the UK had been taking steps to boost the strength and independence of the independent, non-executive directors and had been forcing listed companies down the route of separating the roles of chairman and CEO, the US model had continued to place almost complete power in the hands of the CEO. In the vast majority of US listed corporations, the company continued to be led by a single person who was both chairman and CEO, and who picked his or her own board members on whatever criteria seemed individually appropriate. CEOs tended therefore to appoint outside directors who were likely to share the same values and objectives, who were perhaps likely to contribute to the success of the company, but who were not likely to disagree with or challenge their leader.

This approach seemed to have been justified, as US companies – led by celebrity CEOs – led the TMT (technology, media and telephony) boom at the end of the 20th century. Buoyed by a wave of Y2K[12] spending, this boom also seemed to have created an environment in which some corporate bosses felt they could loot their companies with impunity.

The spectacular financial collapse of 'go-go' tech stocks like Global Crossing, Tyco, WorldCom and, in particular, Enron (which itself led directly to the failure of Arthur Andersen, once a mighty audit firm) were the shocks that convinced US regulators that their system of corporate supervision and governance was broken. The Sarbanes–Oxley Act of 2002, which radically overhauled the US system of corporate governance, particularly focusing on the financial aspects, was the immediate result.

The Sarbanes–Oxley Act (which we will look at in more detail in Chapter 2) was at once more far-reaching, more draconian and, in its detailed application, a significant step forward for corporate governance. It instituted what might be called the 'comply or die' principle, by which those corporations that fail to comply with its requirements face significant corporate financial sanctions as well, potentially, as criminal sanctions for their directors and officers.

# NOTES

1. *Concise Oxford English Dictionary*, 11th edn.
2. See, for instance, Bruce Brown (2003) *The History of the Corporation*, vol. I, BF Communications.
3. The Catholic Church's Benedictine Order was founded in AD 529.
4. The Royal Exchange and London Assurance Corporation Act 1719 forbade any joint stock companies that did not have a royal charter; it was repealed in 1825.
5. The Boston Manufacturing Company was established in 1813.
6. According to Professor Andrew Chambers (2003) *Tottel's Corporate Governance Handbook*, Tottel Publishing, Haywards Heath.
7. Robert Tricker (1984) *Corporate Governance*, Gower, Aldershot.
8. The Committee of Sponsoring Organizations of the Treadway Commission published its *Internal Control – Integrated Framework* report in September 1992.
9. Cadbury Committee (1992) *The Financial Aspects of Corporate Governance* (Cadbury Report), Gee, London.
10. Ibid., Preface.
11. Ian Jones and Michael Pollitt (2003) *Understanding How Issues in Corporate Governance Develop: Cadbury Report to Higgs Review*, December, ESRC, Swindon.
12. The Year 2000 problem stemmed from a belief that computer systems around the world would fail at the point of midnight on 1 January 2000, as their two-digit clocks changed from '99' to '00'. While some organizations recoded applications, many others replaced or upgraded existing IT systems. The absence of spectacular corporate failures on New Year's Day undermined the credibility of tech gurus.

# 2

# Corporate governance in the United States

The statutory framework for corporate governance in the United States is very different from that in the United Kingdom. This difference emerges from the fact that company law, in the United States, exists only at a state level, not a federal one. Most US companies choose to incorporate in Delaware, which has no legal framework for financial reporting or accounting controls and has weak shareholder rights protection. When federal action is needed, the only route that has been available to US regulators has been through securities regulation.

The United States Securities and Exchange Commission (the SEC) exists to 'protect investors, maintain fair, orderly and efficient markets, and facilitate capital formation'.[1] It was established by Congress in 1934, to enforce the Securities Act of 1933 and the Securities Exchange Act of 1934. The SEC makes regulations, or rules, to implement legislation that has been passed by Congress and signed into law by the president. It is these detailed rules (which are subject to review and amendment by the SEC in the ordinary course of business) rather than the original Act itself that are subject to enforcement and with which US listed companies must comply.

## SARBANES–OXLEY (SOX)

The Sarbanes–Oxley Act, sponsored by Senator Paul S Sarbanes and Congressman Michael G Oxley, was signed into US law on 30 July 2002 in response to the series of corporate scandals that followed the bursting of the internet bubble. Global Crossing, Enron and WorldCom were each guilty of destroying significant amounts of shareholder wealth as well as negatively impacting a host of other stakeholders.

The Sarbanes–Oxley Act was probably the most radical and dramatic change to US federal securities laws since the 1930s legislation.

SOX applies to companies that have listings on US exchanges, irrespective of where they are headquartered or what other compliance responsibilities they have, and to organizations that do not have listings but do have significant US-based shareholdings. More specifically, SOX was drafted to apply to all companies that have to file reports with the SEC under the US Securities Exchange Act of 1934, which are therefore termed 'filers'. While a number of the provisions had immediate effect, others were delayed to allow companies preparation time. 'Accelerated filers',[2] larger companies with a total equity of $75 million or more and that are required to file their various SEC returns more quickly than smaller companies (or 'non-accelerated filers'), had stricter SOX compliance deadlines.

The first significant requirement was that every public company has to have an audit committee, which must consist solely of independent directors. This provision had to be met by 26 April 2003.

While the Act lays down other detailed requirements for the governance of organizations (including, in section 806, protection for 'whistle-blowers'), the most widely recognized sections of SOX are 302, 404 and 409.

Section 302 (effective from 29 August 2002) requires the disclosure of all known control deficiencies; section 404 (effective for fiscal years ending after 15 September 2003 for accelerated filers) requires management's annual certification of internal controls and an audit opinion; and section 409 requires the monitoring of operational risk and the real-time reporting of material events.

Sections 802 and 906 are also important, not least because they both introduce significant legal sanctions for non-compliance (the 'or die' aspect of the US corporate governance framework).

## Section 302: Executive certification of financial reports

Section 302 required the CEO and CFO personally to sign quarterly and annual financial reports, certifying that:

1.  they have reviewed the report;

| Section | 302 | 404 | 409 |
| --- | --- | --- | --- |
| Requirement | – Quarterly certification of financial reports<br>– Disclosure of all known control deficiencies<br>– Disclosure of acts of fraud | – Management certification of internal controls (annually)<br>– Independent accountant attests report<br>– Quarterly reviews of changes | – Monitor operational risks<br>– Material event reporting<br>– 'Real-time' implications<br>– four business days allowed for report to be filed |
| Responsibility | – CEO<br>– CFO | – Management<br>– Independent accountant | – Management<br>– Independent accountant |

2. the report does not (to their knowledge) contain any untrue statement or omission of a material fact that might make the financial statements misleading;

3. the financial statements fairly present (to their knowledge) in all respects the financial conditions and results of the company;

4. they, the signing officers,

   a. are responsible for establishing and maintaining internal controls;

   b. have designed the internal controls to ensure that material information is made known to them;

   c. have evaluated the effectiveness of the internal controls for the 90-day period prior to the reporting date;

   d. have presented in the report their conclusions about the effectiveness of the controls as at that date;

5. they have disclosed to the auditors and to the audit committee:

   a. all significant deficiencies in the design or operation of the internal controls;

   b. any fraud that involves management or other employees who have a significant role in the internal controls; and, finally

6.   they have indicated whether or not there have been any significant changes in internal controls, including any corrective actions, since the date of their evaluation.

These provisions made it impossible for either the CEO or the CFO to advance 'I didn't know' or 'No one told me' as a defence in the case of misreported numbers.

## Section 404: Attestation on internal controls

Under SOX section 404 (a), management is required in the annual report to provide an internal control report assessing the effectiveness of the company's internal control over financial reporting and, under section 404 (b), the auditors must provide an attestation report on internal control over financial reporting in the company's annual report; in other words, both management and the company's auditors are required to certify the organization's internal controls.

The SEC has mandated US companies to use a recognized internal control framework that has been developed through a due process, including inviting public comment. One widely used framework is known as the COSO framework or, to give it its own title, the 'Internal Control – Integrated Framework', which contains the recommendations of the Committee of Sponsoring Organizations of the Treadway Commission.[3] The sponsoring organizations included the AICPA, the Institute of Internal Auditors, the Institute of Management Accountants and the American Accounting Association.

The Public Company Accounting Oversight Board (PCAOB),[4] which was created under SOX to oversee the activity of the auditors of public companies in the United States, expected the majority of US listed public companies to adopt the COSO framework. PCAOBUS Auditing Standard No. 2, which dealt with the audit of internal control over financial reporting, therefore assumes that the COSO framework (or one substantially like it) would have been adopted.

The SEC has identified the Turnbull Guidance[5] as a suitable framework for complying with US requirements to report on internal controls over financial reporting, as set out in SOX section 404 and related SEC rules.

The UK Financial Reporting Council (FRC) published, in December 2004, a guide for UK and Irish companies[6] registered with the SEC on the use of the Turnbull Guidance for these purposes.

The role of internal controls in corporate governance is discussed further in Chapter 13.

## Section 906: Individual responsibility for certifying reports

Section 906 made it a criminal offence (punishable by a fine or a prison sentence, or both) to knowingly certify financial reports that are inaccurate.

## Section 802: Criminal penalties for altering documents

One feature of the millennial bursting bubble was the alteration, deletion or disappearance of corporate records. Not surprisingly, SOX made it a criminal offence to fail to retain and protect audit and related documents, including electronic records, and this is one of a number of aspects of SOX responsible for increasing management awareness of the whole issue of IT governance, which has a separate chapter in this book (Chapter 18). Audit records, and all supporting documentation, must now be retained for a minimum of five years.

# REVIEW OF SOX

SOX has been subject to considerable criticism, particularly from those organizations that have had to make substantial investments in updating and strengthening their systems of internal control to enable their officers to comply with the Act.

It's difficult for anyone to argue, cogently, that shareholders' interests were better served in the days when corporate officers could, in effect, allow the numbers to be made up and then file an 'I didn't know' defence.

In May 2007, the SEC issued revised interpretive guidance with respect to section 404. This guidance, which became effective on 27 June 2007, was more risk-based than previously and offered management a form of 'safe harbour' in following this revised guidance. In parallel, PCAOBUS issued Auditing Standard No. 5,[7] which superceded the earlier Standard No.2.

# NYSE CORPORATE GOVERNANCE RULES

Although the press often seems to suggest that US corporate governance starts and finishes with SOX, the fact is that the New York Stock Exchange (NYSE) has its own set of corporate governance rules (often referred to as 'Standards'). These were approved by the SEC on 4 November 2003.

These rules are codified in the NYSE's *Listed Company Manual*.[8] Like the UK's Combined Code, the NYSE Standards pulled together a number of earlier corporate governance requirements into a set of rules.

These rules are not, however, the end of the story: corporations have in addition to comply with SOX requirements on audit and audit committees and with the SEC's Final Rule on 'Management Reports on Internal Control over Financial Reporting and Certification of Disclosure in Exchange Act Periodic Reports' (11 June 2003), which is the SEC's mandatory interpretation of SOX section 404. The US rules are, in one other respect, very different from those of the UK: listed companies must comply with the rules, which are contained in the NYSE Listing Rules and which are, therefore, mandatory, and the NYSE can issue a public reprimand to any company that violates these rules. In contrast to the UK's 'comply or explain' principle, the requirement for a US listed company is that the CEO must annually certify to the NYSE that he or she is not aware of any violation by the company of NYSE Listing Rules.

# OVERSEAS COMPANIES LISTED ON THE NYSE

US listed companies that are primarily listed outside the United States are permitted (with some exceptions) to follow their home country's corporate governance practices; UK companies listing on the NYSE, in other words, will continue following UK corporate governance practices, with the following exceptions, as set out in section 303 of the NYSE Listing Rules:

▌ 303A.06: listed companies must have an audit committee that meets the requirements of the Exchange Act rule 10A-3;

▌ 303A.11: listed companies must disclose any significant ways in which their home corporate governance practices differ from those required under the NYSE standards;

▌ 303A.12(b): listed company CEOs must notify the SEC in writing immediately they become aware of any material non-compliance with section 303.

# NOTES

1.  www.sec.gov.
2.  With effect from 27 December 2005, these definitions changed. A 'large accelerated filer' is an organization with a worldwide market value of $700 million or more; an 'accelerated filer' is one with a market value of between $700 million and $75 million; and a 'non-accelerated filer' is below that limit. Large accelerated filers have to file their annual report with the SEC within 60 days of the year end; accelerated filers have 75 days.
3.  COSO's website can be found at http://www.coso.org. The executive summary of this report is at http://www.coso.org/publications/executive_summary_integrated_framework.htm.
4.  www.pcaobus.org.
5.  The Turnbull Guidance is discussed in detail in Chapter 13.
6.  A copy of this guidance can be downloaded from http://www.frc.org.uk/documents/pagemanager/frc/draft_guide.pdf.
7.  Auditing Standard No. 5 can be downloaded from http://www.pcaob.org/Rules/Rules_of_the_Board/Auditing_Standard_5.pdf.
8.  The manual can be downloaded from www.nyse.com.

# 3

# Corporate governance in the European Union

The OECD Principles of Corporate Governance were first published in 1999, but it wasn't until after the Enron and WorldCom debacles, and the US Sarbanes–Oxley Act (SOX) response in 2002, that most other OECD countries made a determined effort to adopt their own codes of corporate governance. With the exception of the United States, though, individual OECD countries have all adopted corporate governance codes that are designed to work on the 'comply or explain' principle. The SOX, on the other hand, is rules-based and works on a 'comply or be punished' principle. One of the knock-on impacts of SOX is that those companies subject to it are also requiring the partners and suppliers on which they depend to certify conformance to SOX because that gives them greater certainty of ongoing compliance themselves.

The most recent UK legislation (the Companies Act 2006) and revisions to the European Union's (EU's) 8th Company Law Directive also point to greater compulsion – from governments, regulators and justice departments – in governance requirements becoming the norm across the OECD.

The interaction between statutory and non-statutory corporate govern-ance frameworks across multiple countries, and the relationship – both political and professional – between regulators in different jurisdictions, is far more complex than the framework in any single country. There is already substantial guidance to what is a fast-changing topic, and this chapter will not attempt more than an introductory skate across the surface of these oceans.

# OECD CORPORATE GOVERNANCE

Some 29 voluntary corporate governance codes have been adopted within the OECD, mostly since 2002. These include Austria (2002), Canada (2002), France (2002), Germany (Kodex, 2003), Italy (2002), Japan (2001), the Netherlands (Tabaksblatt, 2003) and Switzerland (2002).

The ECGI[1] website contains a list of all the current corporate governance codes of all the countries in the OECD, together with copies of other best-practice guidance documents.

The new OECD Principles of Corporate Governance were published in 2004. These focus primarily on public companies and on developing corporate governance in emerging countries. There are only six high-level principles, each supported by a number of recommendations. The OECD Principles are broader than the United Kingdom's Combined Code, in that they include other issues – such as share registration and share transfer – which are dealt with in the United Kingdom's Listing Rules or statutory regime.

The six section titles of the OECD Principles of Corporate Governance[2] are:

1.  Ensuring the basis for an effective corporate governance framework.

2.  The rights of shareholders and key ownership functions.

3.  The equitable treatment of shareholders.

4.  The role of stakeholders in corporate governance.

5.  Disclosure and transparency.

6.  The responsibilities of the board.

The World Bank is charged with assessing the application of the OECD Principles of Corporate Governance, and these assessments[3] form part of the World Bank and International Monetary Fund (IMF) programme of assessments of countries' legal and regulatory frameworks, the practices and compliances of their listed firms, and identification of economic and financial vulnerability.

# STATUTORY FRAMEWORK FOR CORPORATE GOVERNANCE IN EUROPE

There are many significant differences in corporate law between the United Kingdom and United States, on the one hand, and the countries of continental Europe, on the other.

The UK and US law provides, for instance, for companies to be managed by a unitary board, a single board of directors that is ultimately accountable in law for the actions of the company. Many countries in the EU (such as Germany, the Netherlands, France and Austria) and elsewhere in the OECD (such as Indonesia and Taiwan) have a two-tier board structure, which provides for separate management and supervisory boards. In some countries (eg Germany) this is a statutory structure and cannot be changed by shareholders. Two-tier boards are, to some extent or another, strictly separated, with the supervisory board responsible for supervising and monitoring the executive board. Some European laws also mandate trade union membership of supervisory boards.

It should also be noted that, across the EU, the statutory and legal framework for commerce and corporate governance is primarily a civil code, compared to case law in the United States, the United Kingdom and other members of the OECD. In a case law framework, abstract rules are usually drawn from specific cases, whereas in civil codes abstract rules are first created and then applied to specific cases. As a result, individual cases in a case law environment can lead to changes in the law, whereas in the civil code environment legislation is the primary source of law and the code has primacy until such time as it is changed or repealed. Civil codes clearly provide a different legal context for companies from that of case law, and boards planning to operate in civil code jurisdictions should familiarize themselves with these differences.

In spite of this, the EU sees harmonization of company law and corporate governance (as well as accounting and auditing) across Europe as essential for creating a single market for financial services and products.[4] 'Modernisation of Company Law and Enhancement of Corporate Governance' is a significant EU Commission initiative to: 1) strengthen shareholder rights and third-party protection, with a proper distinction between categories of companies; and 2) foster efficiency and competitiveness of business, with special attention to cross-border issues.

The EU Council has so far issued 12 official company law directives, all of which member states are required to bring into national law. Each of the directives is subject to review, update and amendment.

EU regulation is another, highly specialized area of company law; corporate governance practitioners need to be aware of EU corporate governance regulatory developments, although there is usually no need to take action in respect of amendments to EU directives until they have been incorporated into national law.

# NON-STATUTORY CORPORATE GOVERNANCE IN EUROPE

There are two main corporate governance models in the EU. The first is the traditional, continental European model, in which companies are largely controlled by 'block holders': individuals, groups of individuals or organizations that control most of the votes at a company's annual general meetings. The second is the UK (or 'Anglo-Saxon') model, in which shares in a company are widely owned and there is a broad equity base. This means that corporate governance objectives are different in the Anglo-Saxon world from those in the European one.

Few listed companies in the EU are widely held by dispersed, minority shareholders. Instead, they tend to be controlled by one dominant shareholder – often a family or an individual – that controls the majority of votes (and owning at least 20 per cent would define 'control' in this context), without necessarily owning the majority of the shares. This ownership is achieved through dual share classes, shareholder agreements and complex pyramidal ownership arrangements, in which control is exercised through ownership of at least one other public company. In the United States and the United Kingdom, the corporate governance challenge is to alleviate the conflict in interest between dispersed small shareholders and powerful controlling managers, whereas in Europe (and in much of the rest of the OECD) the issue is aligning the interests of controlling and minority shareholders. The Parmalat scandal is the best example of the extent to which a controlling shareholder can abuse its position to feather its own nest.

While there has been some convergence towards the UK model in respect of protection of minority shareholders and the regulation of takeover bids, there is still considerable difference across Europe in the legal substance of national corporate governance frameworks.

The European Corporate Governance Forum was set up in early 2005, by the European Commission, to pursue the objective of EU-wide coordination of corporate governance developments across the EU as a whole. 'The Commission does not want to enact a European

Code of Corporate Governance', said European Commissioner Charlie McCreevy; 'we see no need for this at present and the adoption of such a code, if it were even possible, would be an inevitable and possibly messy political compromise, which would be unlikely to achieve full information for investors about the key corporate governance rules'.[5] McCreevy described the Forum's priorities: 'a first area of work is to examine the existing national codes of corporate governance in order to determine whether there is convergence – if yes to which extent and if not, to determine whether, and, if so, how convergence could be reached'.

A conclusion of the EU's Barcelona summit in 2002 was that economic efficiency has its basis in solid corporate governance. The drive to achieve it will not abate in the foreseeable future. The Anglo-Saxon model is already well advanced.

The simple truth is that any organization wanting to access the world's largest pool of liquid, available financial capital can only turn to the West. And governance requirements, just like financial reporting requirements, are converging as financial institutions and regulatory bodies drive for increased transparency and ease of comparison across multiple jurisdictions.

# FINANCIAL REPORTING AND AUDIT CONVERGENCE

Corporate governance practitioners need to be aware of the extent to which changes in accounting and audit practices will affect their governance activities.

## Financial reporting

Until recently, the major accounting standards were US GAAP (Generally Accepted Accounting Principles), used by the United States and Canada, UK GAAP, used in the UK and in UK-related economies, and the IAS (International Accounting Standards), used almost everywhere else. Different accounting treatments made it difficult for investors – even where corporations reconciled accounts drawn up in accordance with two (or more) standards – to compare corporate performance both within and across sectors.

As markets converge and geographical borders no longer present the same trade barriers, increasingly there is a need for globally accepted accounting standards. Business needs them, investors are demanding them and accountants are under an obligation to ensure delivery. And that is what is happening.

IAS – renamed IFRS (International Financial Reporting Standards) – was adopted (by EU directive) for all EU listed companies with effect from 2005, and the US Financial Standards Accounting Board (FASB) and the International Accounting Standards Board (IASB) are now working towards convergence of accounting standards. This initiative is expected to finalize a single set of international accounting standards in the near future. The IASB is also working with the Bank of International Settlements (BIS), IOSCO (the International Organization of Securities Commissions) and the Japanese accounting body to drive IFRS into all non-US markets, having already endorsed the use of IFRS (in May 2000) for cross-border reporting.

## Audit requirements

Inevitably, with one set of accounting standards, applied by companies accessing a single international corporate pool of capital, there is also a drive towards a convergence in auditing requirements. While the US Corporate and Auditing Accountability, Responsibility, and Transparency Act of 2002, named the Sarbanes–Oxley Act (SOX) after its sponsors, was a response to a specific set of post-asset bubble circumstances, it did raise the bar for audit standards worldwide, as it mandated board and auditor independence and required management to report (with an audit opinion) on the quality of its internal control over financial reporting.

## UK Companies Act 2004

The UK's Companies (Audit, Investigations and Community Enterprise) Act of 2004 (now being replaced by provisions of the Companies Act 2006) placed a statutory duty on officers and employees (including ex-employees) to provide auditors with information (other than legally privileged information) and explanations in respect of any issue related to their audit of the company's accounts. The directors are required to make a statement that they have disclosed (having taken appropriate steps to ascertain it) all relevant information to the auditors, and making a false statement will be a criminal offence. The UK's Financial Reporting Review Panel (the FRRP), which was originally set up in 1990 to look into instances of corporate accounting non-compliance with UK GAAP, gained new powers to require companies, directors and auditors to provide documents, information and explanations if there might be an accounts non-compliance with relevant reporting requirements.

With the exception of small and medium enterprises, UK companies are now required to make detailed disclosure of non-audit services supplied by their auditors.

For financial years beginning on or after 1 April 2005, UK quoted companies (which includes UK registered companies that are officially listed in an EU state or on either the NYSE or NASDAQ, but not on AIM or OFEX) were required to publish an operating and financial review (OFR). Under the Companies Act 1985 (Operating and Financial Review and Directors' Report etc) Regulations 2005, companies were required to include a fair review of their business in the directors' report and publish an auditor's opinion on the consistency of the OFR and the accounts; a criminal and administrative enforcement regime was also created.

Previously a voluntary report, the OFR was required to reflect the directors' view of the business, with the objective of assisting investors to assess the strategies adopted and the potential for those strategies to succeed. DTI guidance was that the OFR must 'include a description of the resources available to the company, [and] of the principal risks and uncertainties facing the company'.[6]

In the Companies Act 2006, the OFR was replaced by a business review, which is seen as being less onerous than the OFR. Companies still have to gain experience in publishing the business review, which is being promulgated as an opportunity for companies to better inform their shareholders about the operations of the business; the challenge faced by directors is to find an appropriate balance between publishing information to shareholders and protecting the corporate competitive position.

The FRRP, the United Kingdom's Financial Services Authority (FSA) and the UK Revenue & Customs are also in the process of coordinating their investigative activities so as to comply with standards set by the Committee of European Securities Regulators. The FSA retains the power to decide on corrective or punitive action, and it has a range of sanctions available to it.

## EU 8th Company Law Directive

Clearly driven as much by SOX as by its own home-grown corporate disasters, the EU Commission issued a 'Directive on Statutory Audit' in 2004. This directive (sometimes called 'Europe's SOX' or 'SOX-lite') replaced the existing EU 8th Company Law Directive of 1984. It 'clarifies the duties of statutory auditors, provides for their independence and ethical standards, introduces a requirement for external quality assurance, and provides for the public oversight of the audit profession and improved cooperation between oversight bodies in the EU'.[7] The directive, seen as a 'minimum harmonization' proposal for statutory audits within the EU, also provides a basis for international cooperation between EU regulators and those in third countries. 'The Commission believes that co-operation with the PCAOB [the US Public Corporate Accounting Oversight Board] is particularly important because of the global nature of modern capital markets.'

Negotiations between the EU, the US Securities and Exchange Commission (SEC) and the PCAOB have been taking place to try to avoid EU auditors having to register with the PCAOB. In the UK, the Financial Reporting Council (FRC)'s remit was extended to include independent oversight (through its newly set up Professional Oversight Board for Accountancy – POBA) of the UK accounting profession, and the EU established the European Group of Auditors' Oversight Bodies (the EGAOB) in December 2005. EU and US audit rules are now 'quite convergent', following the principles of independent public oversight, audit quality assurance, more frequent auditor rotation and avoiding conflicts of interest.

The adoption of IFRS and the regulatory convergence opens up the opportunity for the widespread formal adoption of the International Standards on Auditing (ISAs). ISAs are published by the International Auditing and Assurance Standards Board (IAASB) and are already incorporated into the national auditing standards in a number of countries.

## NOTES

1.  http://www.ecgi.com.
2.  The OECD Principles of Corporate Governance can be found at http://www.oecd.org/dataoecd/32/18/31557724.pdf.
3.  See the Worldwide Governance Indicators, 1996–2006 (published July 2007), which covers 212 countries and territories across six dimensions of governance: http://info.worldbank.org/governance/wgi2007/.
4.  See: http://ec.europa.eu/internal_market/company/index_en.htm.
5.  Charlie McCreevy, European Commissioner for Internal Market and Services, 20 January 2005.
6.  'Guidance on the OFR and changes to the directors' report', January 2005 by the UK's DTI.
7.  'Proposal by the European Commission for a directive on statutory audit of annual and consolidated accounts', September 2004 by the UK's DTI.

# 4

# Corporate governance in the United Kingdom – the statutory framework

There would be no non-statutory corporate governance framework without the existence of a statutory framework that allows companies to be created, that puts the core requirements and expectations of companies on a statutory basis and that, therefore, makes it possible for companies to have a legal personality, the key requirement that enables them to enter into contracts of any sort.

The UK has had a system of company registration since 1844, when the Joint Stock Companies Act was passed; limited liability for shareholders (other than in insurance companies) has been available since the passage of the Limited Liability Act in 1855, and this protection was extended to insurance companies in 1862.

Although companies initially had to have 25 or more shareholders, this requirement was reduced to seven by the Companies Act of 1856 and finally, in 1992, reduced to only one as a result of the EU's 12th Council Company Law Directive, which required member states to make legal structures available for individuals to trade with limited liability.

Sole proprietorship businesses are unincorporated; their owner has no partners and liability is unlimited. Sole proprietorships are not the subject of corporate governance. The entities that do fall within the scope of the modern corporate governance movement are those corporations in which the management and the shareholders are not the same persons and that have the characteristics described earlier, in Chapter 1. Most often, these corporations have commercial objectives, but they also exist in local government, the not-for-profit sector (political, religious and charitable) and the public–private sector ('quangos').

Partnerships are also a business entity, and they come in three basic forms:

▌ the general partnership, in which all partners share the profits and liabilities of the partnership;

▌ the limited partnership, in which some partners have lessened management responsibility and lessened liabilities; and

▌ the limited liability partnership (LLP), in which all the partners have some form of limited liability.

While these entities are important in the business and non-business spheres (and have key roles to play, as lawyers, accountants, auditors and many other professional organizations), they are not the direct focus of today's corporate governance activity and we will not, therefore, spend much time on them here.

## THE UK LIMITED LIABILITY COMPANY

There are three main types of limited liability corporation in the United Kingdom:

▌ Private company, limited by shares ('limited' or 'ltd'), which means that the liability of the shareholders is limited to the amount either that they have already paid on their shares or that is still due on shares that were issued partly paid. Private limited companies can have one shareholder, one director and a minimum share capital of £1 and, because they are often – but not always – managed by their owners, the need to regulate the relationship between these two groups is not usually a significant one.

▌ Public limited company (PLC), also limited by shares, but with more onerous requirements than a limited company. While a PLC does not have to be listed on a stock exchange (ie quoted), no company can be listed without first becoming a PLC, and (usually for reasons of prestige) unquoted PLCs are not uncommon in the United Kingdom. A PLC has to have at least two shareholders, two directors, a properly qualified company secretary, and share capital of at least £50,000, a quarter of which has to be paid up (ie it must have at least £12,500 in capital when it commences trading). There are a number of other restrictions on what PLCs can do by comparison with private limited companies, and organizations considering this option will usually take professional legal advice as part of their decision-making process. Virtually all the organizations about which corporate governance is concerned will be PLCs.

▌ Private company, limited by guarantee (also 'limited' or 'ltd'), which is a company that does not have shareholders. It has members (who can be individuals or any other legal entity), who each undertake to guarantee the company's debts if it is liquidated. As the amount of the guarantee is usually set at £1 per member, the value of the guarantee is not important. What does matter is that there are no shareholders to whom a dividend can be paid or who might benefit from any form of return of capital to shareholders. As a result, guarantee companies (which are in all ways subject to the Companies Acts) are a common form for voluntary sector and public–private sector partnership organizations. The fact that these organizations either are publicly funded or have public benefit objectives means that they, too, are subject to significant corporate governance expectations.

It should be noted that the law on limited liability companies is such that a group of companies, a conglomerate, can create subsidiary limited liability companies and, if the subsidiaries fail or become insolvent, have no liability as shareholders for their debts. The decision, for instance, to grant credit payment terms to the subsidiary of a listed conglomerate should be made only on the basis of the creditworthiness of that subsidiary on its own merits.

The registration requirements for UK companies are set out in a series of Companies Acts, which have followed a pattern of amending and then replacing previous Acts. UK companies are registered in England and Wales, or in Scotland (all through Companies House, following a very simple procedure), or in Northern Ireland.

# THE COMPANIES ACT 2006

The founding Companies Act of the modern era was passed in 1948. This Act and later developments were consolidated into a new Companies Act in 1985, which itself was further amended and developed in 1989. A further Act, the Companies (Audit, Investigations and Community Enterprise) Act (known as 'C(AICE)'), was passed in 2004.

The DTI had commissioned a fundamental review of company law in March 1998. The Company Law Review (CLR) Steering Group were asked to look at how core company law could be modernized for the 21st century, with a focus on simplicity, cost-effectiveness and efficiency. The CLR presented its findings in 2001, and this led to two White Papers, in 2002 and 2005, and after extensive consultation the Company Law Reform Bill was introduced in November 2005. The resulting Companies Act received royal assent in 2006, and introduction commenced in 2007, with the requirement that all provisions are implemented by 2008.[1] The 2006 Act restated (and therefore replaced) almost all of the provisions of the 1985 Act, as well as the company law provisions of the 1989 Act and the C(AICE) Act; it also codified – gave statutory power to – certain aspects of case law, which are described later in this chapter.

## OVERVIEW OF THE STRUCTURE OF THE COMPANIES ACT 2006[2]

| Part | Summary |
| --- | --- |
| Parts 1 to 7 | The fundamentals of what a company is, how it can be formed and what it can be called. |
| Parts 8 to 12 | The members (shareholders) and officers (management) of a company. |
| Parts 13 and 14 | How companies may take decisions. |
| Parts 15 and 16 | The safeguards for ensuring that the officers of a company are accountable to its members. |
| Parts 17 to 25 | Raising share capital, capital maintenance, annual returns and company charges. |
| Parts 26 to 28 | Company reconstructions, mergers and takeovers. |
| Parts 29 to 39 | The regulatory framework, application to companies not formed under the Companies Acts and other company law provisions. |
| Parts 40 to 42 | Overseas disqualification of directors, business names and statutory auditors. |
| Part 43 | Transparency obligations. |
| Parts 44 to 47 | Miscellaneous and general. |

The 1985 and 1989 Companies Acts are now, for most purposes, of no further interest to ordinary corporate governance practitioners. Of the company law provisions in the 1985 and 1989 Acts, the only ones that remain are those on investigations that go wider than companies (Part 14 of the 1985 Act). The provisions on community interest companies in Part 2 of the C(AICE) Act 2004 also remain in force.

The non-company law provisions in the 1985 and 1989 Acts that remain are:[3]

▍ Part 18 of the 1985 Act (floating charges and receivers (Scotland));

▍ Part 3 of the 1989 Act (powers to require information and documents to assist overseas regulatory authorities);

▍ Sections 112 to 116 of the 1989 Act (provisions about Scottish incorporated charities);

▍ Part 7 of the 1989 Act (provisions about financial markets and insolvency);

▍ Schedule 18 of the 1989 Act (amendments and savings consequential upon changes in the law made by the 1989 Act);

▍ Sections 14 and 15 of the C(AICE) Act 2004 (supervision of accounts and reports); and

▍ Sections 16 and 17 of the C(AICE) Act 2004 (bodies concerned with accounting standards etc).

In non-company law areas the Act makes amendments to other legislation, in particular the Financial Services and Markets Act 2000, and also makes new provision of various kinds. The main areas in which provision of this kind is made are:

▍ overseas disqualification of company directors (Part 40);

▍ business names (Part 41) – replacing the Business Names Act 1985;

▍ statutory auditors (Part 42) – replacing Part 2 of the Companies Act 1989; and

▍ transparency obligations (Part 43) – amending Part 6 of the Financial Services and Markets Act 2000.

# CORE PROVISIONS OF THE COMPANIES ACT 2006

The Companies Act 2006 has some 760 pages and is a subject for lawyers and legal textbooks. The corporate governance practitioner needs to be familiar with the Act, but does not need to be a lawyer. The contents of the Act are set out in Appendix 1, together with every clause reference, and the practitioner should use this appendix to become familiar with the range of issues covered by the Companies Act 2006 and to identify those issues with which greater familiarity may, in certain circumstances, be advisable.

The Companies Act 2006 sets out the legal basis for the formation of a company. A company's constitution is its memorandum and articles of association. The memorandum regulates the external affairs of the company and provides information about the registered office, the objects of the company and the shareholdings. The articles, on the other hand, regulate the internal affairs of the company and provide information about shares, voting, directors and meetings of the company.

Some companies may also have a shareholders' agreement, which in most cases will be drafted to override key provisions of the articles, and all directors of companies should ensure that they are familiar with the memorandum, the articles and any extant shareholders' agreement.

## Memorandum – objects clause

A company has no legal authority to undertake anything outside the objects for which it is incorporated, and these objects are contained in the objects clause of the memorandum. If a company acts outside these objectives, it is acting *ultra vires* (beyond the power). The original reasons for the objects clause were: 1) to protect investors, by ensuring that the company in which they had invested could only do what it had promised to do; and 2) to protect third parties dealing with the company, who would be able to determine from the objects clause whether or not the company could enter into particular arrangements.

This has always been both a governance issue and an issue for individual directors: if the company acts *ultra vires* then the acts are voidable and directors could find themselves personally liable for a breach of duty to the company. For a long time, therefore, companies have ensured that they don't fall foul of the *ultra vires* rule by drawing their objects clauses so widely and in such vague terms that it would be virtually impossible for any of their activities to fall outside them.

The Companies Act 2006 removed this issue: companies are no longer required to specify their objects, and the memorandum has become a formal document recording the position at registration, with the articles being the continuing constitutional document.

## Articles of association

The articles of association contain the detailed rules governing the internal affairs of the company. The 1985 Companies Acts contained model articles in the form of a Table A, and companies usually adopted these model articles with some exclusions and alterations. The new Act does not contain such a table; instead, the Secretary of State is empowered to prescribe model articles separately by regulations and, at the time of writing this book, the Department for Business, Enterprise and Regulatory Reform (formerly the DTI) was in consultation about three sets of model articles of association to be included in the planned Companies (Model Articles) Regulations 2007.[4] These cover:

▌ private companies limited by shares;

▌ public companies;

▌ private companies limited by guarantee.

The model articles – which are designed for use by companies formed and registered under the 2006 Act – for private companies are simpler than those for public companies. The PLC model articles cover:

▌ directors' powers and responsibilities;

▌ decision making by directors;

▌ appointment of directors (including of alternates);

▌ organization of general meetings;

▌ voting at general meetings;

▌ restrictions on members' rights;

▌ class meetings;

▌ issue of shares;

▌ interests in shares and share certificates;

▌ partly paid shares;

- transfer and transmission of shares;

- consolidation of shares;

- distributions;

- capitalization of profits;

- exercise of members' rights;

- communications and administrative arrangements.

# NOTES

1.  See http://www.companiesact.org.uk/.
2.  Drawn from 'Companies Act 2006, Explanatory notes', prepared by the DTI; the detailed table of contents from the Act forms Appendix 1 in this book.
3.  Ibid.
4.  The draft versions of these articles are at http://www.dti.gov.uk/files/file37976.pdf.

# 5

# Corporate governance in the United Kingdom – the non-statutory framework

The United Kingdom has a complex statutory and non-statutory corporate governance framework. The statutory component of this was outlined in the previous Chapter and is contained in a series of Companies Acts. The Companies Act 1948 was the foundational act of the modern era and it, together with all those that followed, has been brought up to date in the Companies Act 2006, which supersedes and substantially replaces all its forerunners.

The Combined Code on Corporate Governance, based on the Cadbury Code (*The Financial Aspects of Corporate Governance*), which was published in 1992 and which has been reviewed, developed and added to, is the basis of the non-statutory regime.

## CADBURY, GREENBURY AND HAMPEL

After the publication of the Cadbury Code, a Working Group on Internal Control was established to provide guidance to companies on how to comply with the Code's Principle 4.5, which dealt with 'reporting on the effectiveness of the company's system of internal control'. This led to the 1994 publication of the Rutteman Report, *Internal Control and Financial Reporting*.

There was controversy and trade union-supported public anger over a pay rise given, in 1995, to Cedric Brown, the CEO of newly privatized British Gas, about pay packages generally for directors of privatized utilities, and about boardroom bonuses at the National Lottery operator, Camelot. The Confederation of British Industry (CBI) appointed a Study Group on Directors' Remuneration, under the chairmanship of Sir Richard Greenbury, to look into this issue. The Greenbury Report, published in July 1995, focused on the directors of UK listed companies and recommended a code of best practice on executive remuneration that was based on the principles of accountability, transparency and linkage of rewards to performance, which included extensive disclosure in annual reports on remuneration and recommended the establishment of a remuneration committee composed of non-executive directors. The majority of these recommendations were included in the Stock Exchange Listing Rules.

Cadbury and Greenbury were responses to issues of public concern, and made recommendations that, if they had been in place earlier, might have prevented the series of abuses, malpractice and fraud that had taken place. They were essentially backward-looking; the Hampel Committee then took a fresh look at corporate governance, particularly at the positive contribution that it could make to corporate success.

The Hampel Committee (Sir Ronald Hampel, the Committee on Corporate Governance) was established (in line with review recommendations contained in the two original Codes) in November 1995 to review the extent to which the Cadbury and Greenbury reports had been implemented and whether their objectives had been met. The Hampel Report stressed that companies should apply the principles of corporate governance 'flexibly, with common sense, and with due regard to companies' individual circumstances. "Box ticking" is neither fair to companies nor likely to be efficient in preventing abuse.'[1] The Hampel Committee made a total of 56 separate recommendations (dealing with corporate governance, the role of directors, directors' remuneration, the role of shareholders, and accountability and audit), which included and endorsed those already contained in the Cadbury and Greenbury codes and which stressed that the pursuit of the principles of corporate governance were more important than complying with sets of prescriptive rules.

The Hampel Committee then drew up what was published, in June 1998, as the Combined Code on Corporate Governance, a non-statutory code that applied to all UK Stock Exchange listed companies, which covered areas relating to the structure and operations of the board, directors' remuneration, accountability and audit, relations with institutional shareholders, and the responsibilities of institutional shareholders. The Combined Code was appended to (but was not part of) Listing Rule 12.43A, which required companies to provide in their annual reports a narrative statement of how they had applied the Code principles and to state that they had complied with the Code provisions or, if not, why not and for what period.

The 1998 Combined Code applied to all UK listed companies from 31 December 1998 until reporting years commencing on or after 1 November 2003, when it was superseded by the revised Combined Code of 2003. The 2003 version was itself reviewed and, after minor amendments, republished in June 2006 to apply to reporting years beginning on or after 1 November 2006.

# TURNBULL

One requirement of the Combined Code requires companies to provide a statement in their annual report on how they have dealt with internal control.[2] There had been confusion over the extent to which internal control should deal with non-financial as well as financial risks, which meant that guidance for companies on how this should be approached was needed. This led to the establishment of the Turnbull Committee (Sir Nigel Turnbull, the Internal Control Working Party of the Institute of Chartered Accountants in England and Wales) in 1998 by the Institute of Chartered Accountants in England and Wales (ICAEW), which then resulted in the Turnbull Report, *Internal Control: Guidance for directors on the Combined Code*, which was first published in September 1999.[3]

Turnbull stressed that the directors were responsible for controlling all risks to the company's business, both financial and non-financial. The Turnbull Report has critical relationships with the Sarbanes–Oxley Act and with the operational risk requirements of Basel 2, and we deal with enterprise risk management in Chapter 12.

# MYNERS

The Combined Code on Corporate Governance is non-statutory; listed companies are not legally compelled (and never have been) to comply with its provisions. The FSA's Listing Rules do, however, require listed companies to provide a narrative description of how they have applied the principles of the Code and to explain where they have not applied any of its provisions, why not.[4]

This is a significant and substantial difference between the basis of UK listed company regulation and that in the United States. UK listed companies are not legally required to comply with the Combined Code; most, though, find it easier to comply than to identify those provisions with which they do not comply and then to attempt to explain why they have decided not to.

HM Treasury has, in parallel with the evolution of the Combined Code, encouraged institutional investors to review their relationship with the companies in which they were invested and improve their investment performance. In March 2000, the Chancellor of the Exchequer commissioned Paul Myners to conduct a review of institutional investment in the United Kingdom and to consider whether there were factors distorting their investment decision making. Myners published a report a year later, in which he recommended that pension fund trustees adopt a series of principles codifying best practice for investment decision making. It included suggestions for the improvement of communication between investors and companies and encouraged institutional investors to consider their responsibilities as owners and how they should exercise their rights on behalf of beneficiaries. He suggested that this code of investment principles should work in the same way as do those of the Combined Code, on a 'comply or explain' basis.

The adoption of the Myners principles was reviewed in 2005 and the review concluded that progress has been 'patchy'. The Treasury decided against making the Myners principles statutory, but committed itself to working with the pension industry to improve conformance quickly.

# HYPERACTIVITY

The period between 1992 and 2001 had seen the publication of four separate corporate governance codes or guidance documents, as well as the Combined Code itself. Companies Acts were passed in 1985, 1989 and 1992, and the only other substantial legislation during this period was the Financial Services and Markets Act 2000. In the next five years, there were reviews of three aspects of the Combined Code, a review of the Turnbull Guidance, a review of companies legislation, the publication of two new Companies Acts and the introduction of regulations relating to directors' remuneration.

## Directors' Remuneration Report Regulations

The Directors' Remuneration Report Regulations[5] were introduced in 2002 to provide statutory support to the powers of shareholders in relation to quoted company[6] directors' pay. The remuneration report must be signed on behalf of the board, is subject to audit by the company's auditors (who must express an opinion as to its compliance with the requirements of the Regulations) and must be approved by the shareholders at the annual general meeting. Note that it is the report that is approved, not the actual remuneration itself, and the Regulations provide that no remuneration entitlement can be made conditional on the passage of the resolution.[7]

The information that must be provided is broken down into two classes, the first of which is not subject to audit and the second of which is. In the first class is information relating to the make-up of the remuneration committee, a statement of the company's remuneration policy, and a detailed statement describing performance conditions attached to any share options or other long-term incentive plan (LTIP), together with a series of graphs demonstrating comparative share performance. It must also contain a statement of the company's policy on directors' service contracts, as well as on notice periods and termination payments, together with specific details about individual service contracts.

The information subject to audit includes all amounts paid to directors, whether in the form of salary, pension, bonus or other amounts, as well as extensive details around share options and LTIPs, and any non-cash elements, including pension benefits, early retirement benefits, etc.

All directors who fail to ensure that their company complies with the regulations ('every person who was a director of the quoted company immediately before the end of the period for laying and delivering accounts and reports for the financial year in question') are individually guilty of an offence and liable to a fine.[8]

## Review of the Combined Code: Higgs, Smith and Tyson

In July 2002 the Department of Trade and Industry (DTI) and HM Treasury instigated a review of the Combined Code following a review of company law.

Derek Higgs produced his report, *Review of the Role and Effectiveness of Non-Executive Directors*, in January 2003. His report included a definition of 'independence' and recommendations for the following: that at least half the directors should be independent non-executive directors; that committees should be entirely non-executive; an expansion of the role of the senior independent director to provide an alternative channel to shareholders and to lead evaluations on the chairman's performance; added emphasis on the process of nominations to the board through a transparent and rigorous process; and evaluation of the performance of the board, its committees and individual directors. His recommendation that the CEO should not go on to become chairman of the same company was not widely welcomed.

At the same time, a group chaired by Sir Robert Smith, working to a brief from the Financial Reporting Council, published *Audit Committees: Combined Code guidance* in January 2003. The Smith Report set out minimum requirements in respect of the constitution and operation of audit committees, recognized that some companies might be too small to comply and would have to explain why, and encouraged others to go beyond the minimum requirements.

Following publication of the Higgs Report in 2003, the DTI commissioned a task force chaired by Dean Laura Tyson of the London Business School to identify ways in which public companies could improve how they identified, recruited, selected and trained individuals to serve in non-executive positions. *The Tyson Report on the Recruitment and Development of Non-Executive Directors* was published in June 2003.

The Higgs and Smith reports had recommended changes in the Combined Code. These recommendations were duly incorporated, and the revised *Combined Code on Corporate Governance* was published in July 2003. It applied to all companies listed on the primary market of the London Stock Exchange for reporting years commencing on or after 1 November 2003 and is still the current version.

In 2004, the Financial Reporting Council (FRC) established the Turnbull Review Group to review Turnbull's *Internal Control: Guidance for directors on the Combined Code* and to determine whether the guidance needed to be updated. Accordingly, *Internal Control: Revised guidance for directors on the Combined Code* was published by the Financial Reporting Council in October 2005 and applied for financial years beginning on or after 1 January 2006. While there were no significant changes, the revised guidance did recommend that boards continue reviewing their risk management activity and identified the need for the company's risk management framework to be interfaced with the requirements to produce an operating and financial review contained in the Companies Act 2004.

The Turnbull Guidance was also recognized (in 2004) as a Securities and Exchange Commission (SEC) approved framework for management to show that they have adequate internal control structures and financial reporting procedures in place in order to comply with section 404 of the Sarbanes–Oxley Act.

Finally, in June 2006, the FRC published yet another revised version of the Combined Code, following a review of the implementation of the 2003 version. This revision addressed an issue around the chairman serving on the remuneration committee (concluding that he could), and around proxy votes.

# SMALLER COMPANIES SECTOR

Companies listed on AIM in the UK are not formally required to comply with the Combined Code. Some choose to do so. The Quoted Companies Alliance (QCA) published, in July 2005, *Corporate Governance Guidance for AIM Companies*, which is based on the Combined Code and is voluntary.

The QCA was formed in 1992 as a reaction to the abolition of the Unlisted Securities Market (USM) and in the belief that there was a role in London for a junior stock market that could be used for entrepreneurial companies to raise equity funding without undertaking the costly and time-consuming requirements for a main market listing.[9]

The QCA is a not-for-profit, membership organization that solely represents the interests of smaller quoted companies on the Main List, AIM and PLUS. The QCA recognizes that smaller quoted companies have a lower level of resources (in both management and finance terms) than their larger counterparts, as well as a narrower shareholder base and lower investor profile, and that these attributes merit a different basis of treatment from that appropriate for larger listed companies.

The QCA has a framework of eight technical and lobbying committees, and has produced guidance specifically for the smaller quoted companies sector on issues such as:

- investor relations guidance;

- guidance for companies on employee share schemes;

- institutional investor guidelines for share incentive schemes;

- guidance on preparing a business review;

- corporate governance guidance for smaller quoted companies;

- corporate governance guidance for AIM companies.

The *QCA Guidance for Smaller Quoted Companies* (which relates primarily to the balance of executive and non-executive directors on the board) and the *QCA Corporate Governance Guidelines for AIM Companies* are discussed at greater length in Chapter 6 and at appropriate points in this book.

# NOTES

1.  Hampel Report (1998) Summary of Conclusions and Recommendations, Final Report, January, Gee, London.
2.  Financial Reporting Council (2006) *Combined Code on Corporate Governance*, Section C.2, FRC, London.
3.  Chapter 13 provides guidance on how Turnbull applies.
4.  See Chapter 6 for an explanation of how the Listing Rules and the Combined Code interact.
5.  The regulations are discussed in detail in Chapter 10, which deals with directors' remuneration.
6.  A quoted company, for the purposes of these Regulations, is one listed in the United Kingdom, listed in an EU state or listed on either the New York or the NASDAQ stock exchange.
7.  Directors' Remuneration Report Regulations 2002, 241A (8).
8.  Directors' Remuneration Report Regulations 2002, 234B (3) and elsewhere.
9.  www.quotedcompaniesalliance.co.uk

# 6

# The Listing Rules and the Combined Code on Corporate Governance

The UK corporate governance framework for listed companies includes the official Listing Rules of the London Stock Exchange. UK quoted companies are listed either on the London Stock Exchange (LSE) or on the Alternative Investment Market (AIM). The Financial Services Authority (FSA) is the United Kingdom's competent authority for listing, is referred to as the UK Listing Authority (UKLA) and maintains the Official List. The current Listing, Prospectus and Disclosure Rules took effect on 1 July 2005 and replaced the older UKLA Sourcebook. These new Rules reflected changes made following the FSA's review of the listing regime and also implemented the EU Prospectus Directive and certain aspects of the EU Market Abuse Directive in the United Kingdom.

The UK Listing Authority Listing Rules are comprehensive and cover all aspects of the listing of a company's shares, from prospectus through to suspension and delisting. In a number of areas, the Listing Rules impose obligations that are in excess of those contained in either the statutory framework or in the Combined Code, and are described as appropriate in the individual chapters of this book. The following table, which is taken from the UKLA website,[1] shows each of the topics covered by the Listing Rules.

| Reference code | Title |
| --- | --- |
| LR 1 | Preliminary |
| LR 2 | Requirements for listing |
| LR 3 | Listing applications |
| LR 4 | Listing particulars for professional securities market and certain other securities |
| LR 5 | Suspending, cancelling and restoring listing |
| LR 6 | Additional requirements for listing for equity securities |
| LR 7 | Listing Principles |
| LR 8 | Sponsors |
| LR 9 | Continuing obligations |
| LR 10 | Significant transactions |
| LR 11 | Related party transactions |
| LR 12 | Dealing in own securities and Treasury shares |
| LR 13 | Contents of circulars |
| LR 14 | Secondary listing of overseas companies |
| LR 15 | Investment entities |
| LR 16 | Venture capital trusts |
| LR 17 | Debt and specialist securities |
| LR 18 | Certificates representing certain securities |
| LR 19 | Securitised derivatives |
| LR App 1 | Relevant definitions |
| LR App 2 | Fees and financial penalty income |
| LR App 3 | List of regulatory information services |
| LR Transchedule | Transitional provisions |

Topic LR 7, the Listing Principles, describes the scope of the Listing Rules:

### LR 7.1.1 – Application
The Listing Principles apply to every listed company with a primary listing of equity securities in respect of all its obligations arising from the listing rules and the disclosure rules and transparency rules.

### LR 7.1.2 – Purpose
The purpose of the Listing Principles is to ensure that listed companies pay due regard to the fundamental role they play in maintaining market confidence and ensuring fair and orderly markets.

**LR 7.1.3**

The Listing Principles are designed to assist listed companies in identifying their obligations and responsibilities under the listing rules and the disclosure rules and transparency rules. The Listing Principles should be interpreted together with relevant rules and guidance which underpin the Listing Principles.

**LR 7.1.4**

The Listing Principles (LR 7.2.1) are as follows:

Principle 1   A listed company must take reasonable steps to enable its directors to understand their responsibilities and obligations as directors.

Principle 2   A listed company must take reasonable steps to establish and maintain adequate procedures, systems and controls to enable it to comply with its obligations.

Principle 3   A listed company must act with integrity towards holders and potential holders of its listed equity securities.

Principle 4   A listed company must communicate information to holders and potential holders of its listed equity securities in such a way as to avoid the creation or continuation of a false market in such listed equity securities.

Principle 5   A listed company must ensure that it treats all holders of the same class of its listed equity securities that are in the same position equally in respect of the rights attaching to such listed equity securities.

Principle 6   A listed company must deal with the FSA in an open and co-operative manner.

While Principles 1 and 2 are reflected in the Combined Code, the other four principles – which relate very specifically to how a listed company must behave towards current and potential future shareholders and to the FSA, the market regulator – are not.

# SANCTIONS AVAILABLE TO THE UKLA

The key sanctions available to the FSA include fines and, more radically, the suspension of a company's listing. Suspension means that the company's shares can no longer be traded. The Listing Rules set out the basis on which the FSA may suspend a listing:

**LR 5.1.1**
(1) The FSA may suspend, with effect from such time as it may determine, the listing of any securities if the smooth operation of the market is, or may be, temporarily jeopardised or it is necessary to protect investors.

**LR 5.1.2 Examples of when FSA may suspend**
Examples of when the FSA may suspend the listing of securities include (but are not limited to) situations where it appears to the FSA that:

(1)   the issuer has failed to meet its continuing obligations for listing; or

(2)   the issuer has failed to publish financial information in accordance with the listing rules; or

(3)   the issuer is unable to assess accurately its financial position and inform the market accordingly; or

(4)   there is insufficient information in the market about a proposed transaction.

# REQUIREMENT TO COMPLY WITH THE COMBINED CODE

The Listing Rules require, in LR 9.8.6, listed companies to include a statement as to their compliance with the Combined Code. Specifically, the annual report must include:

(5)   a statement of how the listed company has applied the principles set out in Section 1 of the Combined Code, in a manner that would enable shareholders to evaluate how the principles have been applied.

(6)   a statement as to whether the listed company has:

(a)   complied throughout the accounting period with all relevant provisions set out in Section 1 of the Combined Code; or

(b)   not complied throughout the accounting period with all relevant provisions set out in Section 1 of the Combined Code and if so, setting out:

   (i)    those provisions, if any it has not complied with;

   (ii)   in the case of provisions whose requirements are of a continuing nature, the period within which, if any, it did not comply with some or all of those provisions; and

   (iii)  the company's reasons for non-compliance; and

(7)   a report to the shareholders by the Board which contains all the matters set out in LR 9.8.8 R.

The matters referred to in (7) relate to directors' remuneration, which is dealt with in Chapter 10 of this book.

# THE COMBINED CODE ON CORPORATE GOVERNANCE

The current version of the United Kingdom's Combined Code on Corporate Governance was published by the Financial Reporting Council (FRC) in June 2006, following minor revisions to the earlier version, which had been published on 23 July 2003. This revised Code applied to financial reporting years beginning on or after 1 November 2006; the July 2003 version applied to financial reporting years beginning prior to 31 October 2006.

The 2003 version had replaced the earlier 1998 Code, and incorporated (as guidance) the more recent work done by the Higgs review of non-executive directors and the Smith review of audit committees. The clauses in the 1998 Code that related to disclosure of executive pay were withdrawn, because they had been superseded by the Directors' Remuneration Report Regulations 2002, which require the directors to prepare a remuneration report. The review of implementation of the 2003 Code led to relatively minor changes around the eligibility of the chairman to serve on the remuneration committee and around proxy votes, both of which are dealt with in the appropriate chapters of this book.

The 2006 Code[2] consists of:

1.  the Preamble, containing introductory and general principles;
2.  Section 1, setting out requirements for companies and directors;
3.  Section 2, setting out requirements for institutional shareholders;
4.  three schedules, dealing with:

    i.    performance-related pay;

    ii.   liability of non-executive directors;

    iii.  disclosure of corporate governance arrangements.

The three sets of guidance and good practice that were included in the 2003 version of the Combined Code were excluded from the 2006 version and published separately, on the grounds that they had no formal status. These good-practice guides are:

▪ Turnbull Guidance on internal control (2005);[3]

▪ Smith Guidance on audit committees (2005);[4]

▪ Higgs Report and guidance for the chairman and non-executive directors (2003).[5]

The Combined Code looks like a simpler document than it actually is. It contains 43 principles (divided into main principles and supporting principles, both of which are equally important) and 48 provisions.

As the Listing Rules make clear, listed companies have to show how they have complied with Section 1 of the Combined Code. Schedule 2 applies to institutional shareholders, and the guidance and good-practice reports are exactly that; compliance with them is not mandated by the Listing Rules.

The 'comply or explain' principle on which the earlier version of the Combined Code was based had changed by the time of the publication of this revision. While the earlier versions of the Code had contained only provisions, the 2003 and 2006 versions contained both principles and provisions. The current Listing Rules reflect clause 4 of the Preamble to the 2006 Combined Code, which says:

> The Code contains main and supporting principles and provisions. The existing Listing Rules require listed companies to make a

disclosure statement in two parts in relation to the Code. In the first part of the statement, the company has to report on how it applies the principles in the Code. In future this will need to cover both main and supporting principles. The form and content of this part of the statement are not prescribed, the intention being that companies should have a free hand to explain their governance policies in the light of the principles, including any special circumstances applying to them which have led to a particular approach. In the second part of the statement the company has either to confirm that it complies with the Code's provisions or – where it does not – to provide an explanation. This 'comply or explain' approach has been in operation for over ten years and the flexibility it offers has been widely welcomed both by company boards and by investors. It is for shareholders and others to evaluate the company's statement.

In other words, quoted companies must comply (LR 9.8.6 (5)) with the principles and supporting principles (providing a narrative statement of how they have done so) and either confirm or deny (LR 9.8.6 (6)) that they have complied with the provisions. The 'comply or explain' approach is now, in effect, limited to the provisions.

The Combined Code does go on to stress that 'departures from the Code should not be automatically treated as breaches'.[6]

The 2006 Code applies to companies listed on the UK Stock Exchange, primarily to those in the FTSE 350 ('some of the provisions do not apply to companies below FTSE 350'[7]). The Code also recognizes that some of the requirements might be too onerous for smaller or more recently listed companies. The Quoted Companies Alliance (QCA)[8] has published a booklet,[9] in August 2004, to provide guidance for smaller (non-FTSE 350) companies on compliance with the 2003 Combined Code, and this booklet, with an addendum to deal with the minor changes in the 2006 version of the Code, is still valid.

The Combined Code does not apply to AIM companies, as they are not part of the Official List. Some AIM companies voluntarily follow the requirements of the Combined Code. The QCA has developed an alternative code for AIM companies, which is titled *Corporate Governance Guidelines for AIM Companies*. This code, now in its comprehensive second edition, provides an admirably simple and clear set of guidelines.[10] These guidelines have 11 principles, summarized below:

1.  There should be a formal schedule of matters reserved for the board (and Appendix A to the QCA Guidelines proposes the contents of such a schedule).

2.  The board should be supplied with timely information.

3.  There should, at least annually, be a review of the internal control framework.

4.  The roles of chairman and CEO should not be exercised by the same individual.

5.  A company should have at least two independent non-executive directors, one of whom may be the chairman (and Appendix B lists factors that might impair a director's independence).

6.  All directors should be submitted for re-election at regular intervals.

7.  There should be an audit committee (ICSA model terms of reference are at Appendix C of the QCA Guidelines).

8.  There should be a remuneration committee (ICSA model terms of reference are at Appendix D of the QCA Guidelines).

9.  There should be a nomination committee (ICSA model terms of reference are at Appendix E of the QCA Guidelines).

10. There should be dialogue with shareholders.

11. Companies should publish annually a statement explaining how they comply with the QCA Guidelines.

The QCA recommends that these guidelines should represent a 'floor' for corporate governance, and that companies should wherever possible and practical go beyond them.

# NOTES

1.  http://fsahandbook.info/FSA/html/handbook/LR/9/Annex1.
2.  A copy of the 2006 version of the Combined Code can be downloaded from http://www.frc.org.uk/documents/pagemanager/frc/Combined %20Code%20June%202006.pdf.
3.  The Turnbull Guidance is available from http://www.frc.org.uk/ corporate/internalcontrol.cfm.
4.  The October 2005 version of the Smith Guidance is available from http://www.frc.org.uk/documents/pagemanager/frc/Smith%20 Report%202005.pdf.

5.  The January 2003 version of the Higgs Report (published by the FRC in June 2006) is available from http://www.frc.org.uk/documents/pagemanager/frc/Suggestions%20for%20good%20practice%20from%20the%20Higgs%20Report%20June%202006.pdf.
6.  Combined Code 2006, Preamble, para 7.
7.  Combined Code 2006, Preamble, para 6.
8.  For more information about the QCA, see Chapter 5.
9.  *Guidance for Smaller Quoted Companies*, available from www.quotedcompaniesalliance.co.uk.
10.  *Corporate Governance Guidelines for AIM Companies*, 2nd edn, June 2007, available from www.quotedcompaniesalliance.co.uk.

# 7

# Duties of directors

The Commonwealth Association for Corporate Governance (CACG)[1] has proposed that there are 10 directoral duties. These duties are founded on three governance values: accountability, probity and transparency. The 10 duties are:

1.  the duty of legitimacy (operating within the law);

2.  the duty of upholding the director's primary loyalty (which is to the company);

3.  the duty of upholding the director's primary role (which is to help the company succeed, while remaining prudent);

4.  the duty of holding the company in trust (fiduciary duty);

5.  the duty of ensuring critical review of proposals to the board;

6.  the duty of ensuring directoral care (in decision making);

7.  the duty of upholding the three governance values (as above);

8.  the duty of upholding the rights of minority shareholders;

9.  the duty of ensuring corporate social responsibility;

10. the duty of ensuring board learning, development and communication.

These 10 directoral duties may, over the next few years, acquire considerable international support. From the UK perspective, they certainly represent good practice. However, the UK corporate governance framework is more specific than what is contained in these 10 directoral duties.

# WHAT ARE DIRECTORS?

Directors of companies have specific duties and responsibilities; the chairman, chief executive and company secretary are, from a governance perspective, the key roles in a company. Non-executive and executive directors are held to have different responsibilities, but from the perspective of the Companies Act 2006, all directors are equal. There is no difference, in law, between an executive director and a non-executive director.[2] In fact, section 250 says that 'in the Companies Acts "director" includes any person occupying the position of director, by whatever name called'.

The role of 'shadow directors' has also been clarified and enshrined in statute in section 251: 1) 'In the Companies Acts "shadow director", in relation to a company, means a person in accordance with whose directions or instructions the directors of the company are accustomed to act.' 2) 'A person is not to be regarded as a shadow director by reason only that the directors act on advice given by him in a professional capacity.' An example of a shadow director would be a major shareholder whose instructions the directors would always obey, without independently using their judgement. For many purposes of the Companies Act and the Insolvency Act,[3] shadow directors are deemed to be directors and can be liable for breach of the duties imposed on directors in the same way as any other director.

It is particularly important for public–private partnership boards that the capacity and role of 'observers' from funding agencies are clarified and, for this, specialist legal advice may be necessary: there are many circumstances in which such people might be classified as shadow directors (including, for instance, expressing a requirement that the board do X or Y in line with the policy of the funding body) and, as such, be subject to exactly the same requirements and potential penalties as those directors who have been formally appointed.

# FIDUCIARY DUTIES

It is widely understood that directors have a fiduciary duty to their company. But what is a 'fiduciary duty'? A fiduciary is 'a person who holds a position of trust with respect to someone else'.[4] A fiduciary duty can be thought of as the highest standard of care imposed at either equity or law. Fiduciaries are expected to be extremely loyal to the person to whom they owe the duty (the 'principal'): they must not put their personal interests before this duty and must not profit from their position as fiduciaries, unless the principal consents. The fiduciary relationship is highlighted by good faith, loyalty and trust, and the word itself derives from the Latin *fides*, meaning faith, and *fiducia*, meaning trust.

When a fiduciary duty is imposed, equity requires a stricter standard of behaviour than the comparable tortious[5] duty of care at common law. It is said that fiduciaries have a duty not to be in a situation where personal interests and fiduciary duty conflict, a duty not to be in a situation where their fiduciary duty conflicts with another fiduciary duty, and a duty not to profit from their fiduciary position without the express knowledge and consent of the principal. A fiduciary cannot have a conflict of interest.

Shareholders appoint directors. A fiduciary obligation therefore exists whenever one person (the shareholder) places special trust and confidence in another person (the director) and relies upon that person, the fiduciary, to exercise his or her discretion or expertise in acting for the shareholder; and the fiduciary knowingly accepts that trust and confidence and thereafter undertakes to act on behalf of the shareholder by exercising his or her, the fiduciary's, own discretion and expertise.

The concept of the fiduciary duties of directors is based on the concept that a director is in a special position of responsibility in relation to the company and to its shareholders. Directors are therefore held to a higher standard of responsibility than most, which can lead to liability even where they have acted honestly. Directors must act in good faith in the best interests of the company. They must avoid conflicts of interest. They also have a duty not to profit from their position, for example by taking business opportunities that came to them through the company, even if the company does not want to take the opportunities itself. At its most extreme, the duty means that a director cannot receive any payment from the company for acting as a director. However, 'breaches' of these duties can for the most part be approved by shareholders, and most companies, in their articles of association, specifically allow directors to be paid.

These fiduciary duties have long existed in common law, in both the United Kingdom and the United States. They have recently been given statutory support in the United Kingdom.

# STATUTORY PROVISIONS RELATING TO COMPANY DIRECTORS

Part 10 of the Companies Act 2006 sets out statutory requirements in respect of company directors. The Insolvency Act 1986 identifies specific obligations on directors when their company is insolvent or likely to become insolvent, but, as this book is about the governance of 'going concern' companies, those duties are not explored here. It should also be noted that the Companies Act is not alone in identifying directors' duties: other requirements are contained in health and safety legislation, tax legislation, and data protection, consumer protection and many other forms of regulation.

There will also be requirements imposed by the law of foreign jurisdictions in which the company does business. Directors need to make themselves aware of the myriad laws to which they must answer; one way of doing this is to have a matrix of legal requirements developed (perhaps by the company secretary, otherwise by the company's legal advisers) that identifies all the laws under which directors are answerable and thereby puts the directors in a position to establish a methodology for ensuring compliance.

This book, however, is concerned with the specific issues of directors' responsibilities in respect of the overall governance of the organization, rather than with those responsibilities that arise out of other matters.

So, the Companies Act says that all companies are required to have directors, one of whom must be a natural person. Public company director appointments must be voted on individually (section 160), and there are strict rules about the details that must be kept of every director. Directors may be removed by the members of the company (section 168).

The fiduciary duties of directors are set out, for the first time, in the Companies Act 2006. They previously existed as part of common law. They are clearly stated in the Act, and the key parts of the relevant sections are transcribed below:[6]

### 171 Duty to act within powers
A director of a company must –

(a)   act in accordance with the company's constitution, and

(b)   only exercise powers for the purposes for which they are conferred.

### 172 Duty to promote the success of the company
(1)   A director of a company must act in the way he considers, in good faith, would be most likely to promote the success of the company for the benefit of its members as a whole, and in doing so have regard (amongst other matters) to –

(a)   the likely consequences of any decision in the long term,

(b)   the interests of the company's employees,

(c)   the need to foster the company's business relationships with suppliers, customers and others,

(d)   the impact of the company's operations on the community and the environment,

(e)   the desirability of the company maintaining a reputation for high standards of business conduct, and

(f)   the need to act fairly as between members of the company.

### 173 Duty to exercise independent judgment

(1)   A director of a company must exercise independent judgment.

(2)   This duty is not infringed by his acting –

(a)   in accordance with an agreement duly entered into by the company that restricts the future exercise of discretion by its directors, or

(b)   in a way authorised by the company's constitution.

### 174 Duty to exercise reasonable care, skill and diligence

(1)   A director of a company must exercise reasonable care, skill and diligence.

(2)   This means the care, skill and diligence that would be exercised by a reasonably diligent person with –

(a)   the general knowledge, skill and experience that may reasonably be expected of a person carrying out the functions carried out by the director in relation to the company, and

(b)   the general knowledge, skill and experience that the director has.

### 175 Duty to avoid conflicts of interest

(1)   A director of a company must avoid a situation in which he has, or can have, a direct or indirect interest that conflicts, or possibly may conflict, with the interests of the company.

(2)   This applies in particular to the exploitation of any property, information or opportunity (and it is immaterial whether the company could take advantage of the property, information or opportunity).

(3)   This duty does not apply to a conflict of interest arising in relation to a transaction or arrangement with the company.

(4)   This duty is not infringed –

(a)   if the situation cannot reasonably be regarded as likely to give rise to a conflict of interest; or

(b)   if the matter has been authorised by the directors.

(5)   Authorisation may be given by the directors –

(a)   where the company is a private company and nothing in the company's constitution invalidates such authorisation, by the matter being proposed to and authorised by the directors; or

(b)   where the company is a public company and its constitution includes provision enabling the directors to authorise the matter, by the matter being proposed to and authorised by them in accordance with the constitution.

(6)   The authorisation is effective only if –

(a)   any requirement as to the quorum at the meeting at which the matter is considered is met without counting the director in question or any other interested director, and

(b)   the matter was agreed to without their voting or would have been agreed to if their votes had not been counted.

(7)   Any reference in this section to a conflict of interest includes a conflict of interest and duty and a conflict of duties.

## 176 Duty not to accept benefits from third parties
(1)   A director of a company must not accept a benefit from a third party conferred by reason of –

(a)   his being a director, or

(b)   his doing (or not doing) anything as director.

(2)  A 'third party' means a person other than the company, an associated body corporate or a person acting on behalf of the company or an associated body corporate.

(3)  Benefits received by a director from a person by whom his services (as a director or otherwise) are provided to the company are not regarded as conferred by a third party.

(4)  This duty is not infringed if the acceptance of the benefit cannot reasonably be regarded as likely to give rise to a conflict of interest.

(5)  Any reference in this section to a conflict of interest includes a conflict of interest and duty and a conflict of duties.

### 177 Duty to declare interest in proposed transaction or arrangement

(1)  If a director of a company is in any way, directly or indirectly, interested in a proposed transaction or arrangement with the company, he must declare the nature and extent of that interest to the other directors.

(2)  The declaration may (but need not) be made –

(a)  at a meeting of the directors, or

(b)  by notice to the directors in accordance with –

(i)  section 184 (notice in writing), or

(ii)  section 185 (general notice).

(3)  If a declaration of interest under this section proves to be, or becomes, inaccurate or incomplete, a further declaration must be made.

(4)  Any declaration required by this section must be made before the company enters into the transaction or arrangement.

(5)  This section does not require a declaration of an interest of which the director is not aware or where the director is not aware of the transaction or arrangement in question. For this purpose a director is treated as being aware of matters of which he ought reasonably to be aware.

(6)  A director need not declare an interest –

(a)  if it cannot reasonably be regarded as likely to give rise to a conflict of interest;

(b)    if, or to the extent that, the other directors are already aware of it (and for this purpose the other directors are treated as aware of anything of which they ought reasonably to be aware); or

(c)    if, or to the extent that, it concerns terms of his service contract that have been or are to be considered –

(i)    by a meeting of the directors, or

(ii)   by a committee of the directors appointed for the purpose under the company's constitution.

A failure to declare an interest is an offence (and section 182 provides the detail that supports the duty set out in section 177 above) punishable by a fine.

The Companies Act also has specific provisions designed to ensure that members approve transactions between companies and directors, as well as directors' loans and quasi-loans, and credit transactions of any sort, as long as the value of the transaction (or aggregated transactions) does not exceed a *de minimis* level set in the Act for each type of transaction. These provisions do not include an individual's normal business expenses (section 204) or expenditure on defending proceedings (unless, of course, the defence fails, in which case the director concerned becomes liable for the amount).

It should also be noted that, under section 232, 'any provision that purports to exempt a director of a company (to any extent) from any liability that would otherwise attach to him in connection with any negligence, default, breach of duty or breach of trust in relation to the company is void' – directors cannot avoid personal liability for failure to perform their duties properly, and there are strict rules governing the provision, by the company, of officers' and directors' insurance.

## MEETINGS OF DIRECTORS

All companies must ensure that minutes are made of all meetings[7] of their directors (section 248), and these records must be kept for a minimum of 10 years from the date of the meeting. Under section 249, minutes of meetings (if authenticated by the chairman either of the meeting or of the subsequent meeting) are legal evidence that the meeting took place, that it was duly held and convened, and that all decisions and appointments were duly made.

# DELEGATION OF POWERS

The directors can delegate all or some of the powers of management to a management or executive committee, or to a managing director or chief executive (CEO). Most usually, directors delegate to the CEO the powers that are required for the delivery of an approved business plan. Certain rights are usually reserved to the board, and there should be a formal board resolution that sets out, unambiguously, what these are. Any list of matters[8] reserved to the board (in respect of either the company or the group, or both) might include:

▌ strategic plans and any decisions that may significantly impact future profitability;

▌ any decisions to enter, withdraw from or significantly modify any area or sector of business or market sector;

▌ any decisions related to the acquisition or disposal of assets (including shares in other businesses) above a certain specified limit, or where the impact of such a disposal may have an impact above a specified limit;

▌ investments or capital projects above a specified (fully costed) sum;

▌ all contracts that are above a certain value (multi-year contracts valued at the total exposure over the lifetime of the contract);

▌ any significant contracts (or contracts which the board is likely to consider significant) that are not caught elsewhere;

▌ all decisions relating to borrowings, whether new borrowings or changes in the terms of existing borrowings;

▌ appointment or removal of auditors or of other professional advisers;

▌ authorization of all policy statements, whether risk management, treasury, information security, health and safety, environment, quality, etc, and of any changes and amendments to them;

▌ all delegation of authority to executive directors (which would usually be contained in a job description or similar document that sets out clearly what the authority levels of a specific position are);

▌ approval of the company's financial authorization schedule (the schedule that sets out financial authorization limits in respect of the company's day-to-day business) and any amendments to it;

- all decisions related to any proposed changes to the memorandum or articles of association and any other company constitutional documents;

- any matter that has to be dealt with by way of an ordinary or special resolution that is to be put to the shareholders;

- terms of reference (and changes to them) for all board subcommittees, particularly the audit, nomination and remuneration committees, and membership and appointment of the chairman of each such sub-committee;

- approval of the internal control framework, and any changes to it;

- any decision to appoint or remove the chairman, a director or company secretary, or the head of the internal audit function, and any decisions related to their contracts with the company, including their remuneration;

- any transaction in which a director might be interested, whether directly or indirectly;

- the adoption and approval of annual accounts, the directors' report, the directors' remuneration report and any other financial documents that will be made public;

- decisions on anything that is likely to generate significant publicity, particularly of a negative nature.

The Quoted Companies Alliance, in Appendix A of their *QCA Corporate Governance Guidelines for AIM Companies*, also provides a recommended schedule of matters that should be reserved to the board.[9]

# NOTES

1. The CACG involves corporate governance practitioners from the 54 members of the Commonwealth, and is supported by both China and the United States.
2. It is not unusual for this fact to become clear to non-executive directors only at the point at which their company has become potentially insolvent; the Insolvency Act 1986 is crystal clear about what is expected of directors and about the sanctions that face any director who fails to ensure the company takes appropriate steps to protect its creditors at the point at which it is unable to pay its creditors as and when they fall due.

3.  This book deals specifically with the governance of companies that are 'going concerns'. At the point that a company becomes insolvent (either because its liabilities exceed its assets or, more critically, when it can no longer pay its debts as and when they fall due), the duties of directors change significantly and the protection of the creditors becomes their primary concern. Directors must take professional advice as soon as the possibility of insolvency becomes apparent.
4.  *Shorter Oxford English Dictionary*, 5th edn.
5.  'Wrongful' – *Shorter Oxford English Dictionary*, 5th edn; the word, in the legal sense, has the added meaning that dishonest, unfair or untruthful actions are unacceptable.
6.  These sections have been abridged in this section, and readers are advised to refer to the Act itself for the authoritative text.
7.  'All meetings' includes formal board meetings as well as meetings of any of the board's subcommittees.
8.  And this list is neither exhaustive nor exclusive!
9.  See Chapter 6 for more information on the QCA Code.

# 8

# The board

Section 1 of the 2006 Combined Code lists seven principles that should apply to company directors. These principles should be understood in conjunction with the requirements contained in the Companies Act 2006, which were described in Chapter 7. The seven principles deal with:

- A.1: the board;
- A.2: the chairman and chief executive;
- A.3: board balance and independence;
- A.4: appointments to the board;
- A.5: information and professional development;
- A.6: performance evaluation;
- A.7: re-election.

The main principles, and key issues around each principle, are set out below.

## A.1: THE BOARD

'Every company should be headed by an effective board, which is collectively responsible for the success of the company.'[1]

The Code describes in admirably clear terms the role of the unitary board of a company:

The board's role is to provide entrepreneurial leadership of the company within a framework of prudent and effective controls which enables risk to be assessed and managed. The board should set the company's strategic aims, ensure that the necessary financial and human resources are in place for the company to meet its objectives and review management performance. The board should set the company's values and standards and ensure that its obligations to its shareholders and others are understood and met.

This requirement is much broader and more comprehensive than the role that is still often argued for in the United States, which is that the board exists to hire and fire the CEO and otherwise to keep out of his or her way. Such an approach is at odds with the UK Code requirements as well as with the Companies Act 2006.

While the Companies Act does not differentiate between executive and non-executive directors, it is a common arrangement, and the Combined Code describes clearly the role of the non-executives:

non-executive directors should constructively challenge and help develop proposals on strategy. Non-executive directors should scrutinise the performance of management in meeting agreed goals and objectives and monitor the reporting of performance. They should satisfy themselves on the integrity of financial information and that financial controls and systems of risk management are robust and defensible. They are responsible for determining appropriate levels of remuneration of executive directors and have a prime role in appointing, and where necessary removing, executive directors, and in succession planning.

In order to ensure that non-executives are effective in this role, the Combined Code suggests that there should be a senior non-executive director,[2] other than the chairman, and that the non-executives should meet from time to time without the executives, and at least once a year without the chairman. Directors who dissent from an action, or who have concerns on any issue, are expected to require that this be included in the company minutes (which, under the Companies Act are, if approved by the directors and signed, the valid record of a meeting).

# A.2: THE CHAIRMAN AND CHIEF EXECUTIVE

There should be a clear division of responsibilities at the head of the company between the running of the board and the executive responsibility for the running of the company's business. No one individual should have unfettered powers of decision.

This is one of the significant differences between corporate governance structures in the United States and in the United Kingdom. The US unitary board is usually chaired by the CEO of the company. That is extremely unusual in the United Kingdom and is against principle A.2.1, which is explicit that the 'roles of chairman and chief executive should not be exercised by the same individual. The division of responsibilities between the chairman and chief executive should be clearly established, set out in writing and agreed by the board.'

More than that, the chairman should meet the Code's independence criteria,[3] and should not previously have been the CEO of the company. Principle A.2.2 does recognize that, from time to time, there may be good reasons for doing this and so it says that such appointments should only be made after consultation with major shareholders.

The chairman, according to principle A.2, is responsible for:

leadership of the board, ensuring its effectiveness on all aspects of its role and setting its agenda. The chairman is also responsible for ensuring that the directors receive accurate, timely and clear information. The chairman should ensure effective communication with shareholders. The chairman should also facilitate the effective contribution of non-executive directors in particular and ensure constructive relations between executive and non-executive directors.

The Higgs Suggestions for Good Practice, which are included in the Combined Code, expand on these principles. They are clear and concise and, because they should be read and studied in the original text by all directors who are interested in better governance, I am not going to provide extensive commentary on them here.

The Higgs guidance on the role of the chairman stresses the role of the chairman in setting the overall tone for the board, whether in terms of its integrity or of its constructive and open debate allied to effective decision making. The chairman must manage the board and develop a team that is made up of both executive and non-executive directors and that has appropriate induction for new members and development arrangements for all directors.

Above all, the chairman is responsible for enabling the board to reach meaningful, effective strategic decisions: 'agendas should be forward looking and concentrate on strategic matters rather than formulaic approvals of proposals which can be the subject of appropriate delegated powers to management'.

# A.3: BOARD BALANCE AND INDEPENDENCE

The main principle here is that the board should include a balance of executive and non-executive directors (with a particular emphasis on independent non-executive directors), in order to ensure that the board's decision making is not dominated by a single individual or by a clique of dominant individuals. As a UK board could easily include three or four executive directors, in addition to the CEO and CFO, this requirement could lead to a large and unwieldy board.[4] The Combined Code advises against allowing the board to be so big as to be unwieldy. The guidance is that the board should be of sufficient size for the balance of skills and experience around the boardroom table to be appropriate for the requirements of the business, and so that changes to the board's composition (whether through retirement, illness or resignation in the normal course of events) can be managed without undue disruption.

The Combined Code also recognizes that a board with a preponderance of non-executive directors is unlikely to be as effective as a better balanced one. Therefore, to ensure that power and information are not concentrated in the hands of one or two individuals, there should be a strong presence on the board of both executive and non-executive directors. An appropriate balance will also enable the board to select different individuals as chairmen of the nomination, audit and remuneration committees and allow each committee to have an appropriate number of members.[5]

The Combined Code provides specific guidance (A.3.1) that an independent director is someone who is 'independent in character and judgement' and who does not have relationships that might compromise that independence.[6] The independence tests are whether or not the director:

▊ has been an employee of the company or group within the last five years;

▊ has, or has had within the last three years, a material business relationship with the company either directly or as a partner, shareholder, director or senior employee of a body that has such a relationship with the company;

▊ has received or receives additional remuneration from the company apart from a director's fee, participates in the company's share option or a performance-related pay scheme, or is a member of the company's pension scheme;

▊ has close family ties with any of the company's advisers, directors or senior employees;

▊ holds cross-directorships or has significant links with other directors through involvement in other companies or bodies;

▊ represents a significant shareholder; or

▊ has served on the board for more than nine years from the date of his or her first election.

It is recommended that the board should assess the independence of its non-executives annually (but not the chairman, who, although his or her independence should be established prior to appointment, is considered no longer to be independent after appointment),[7] and that at least half the board should be independent non-executive directors (A.3.2).[8]

One of the independent non-executive directors should be appointed to the role of senior independent director (A.3.3). This person should be available to shareholders (or to the other directors) if they have concerns that they have not been able to resolve through the normal channels (ie through the chairman, CEO or CFO). This principle seems to create an alternative nexus of power in the boardroom and has therefore been resisted by many. While it may bring some tensions, the logic behind the principle is the inexorable one that 'the normal channels' can sometimes be more uninterested in the fears and concerns of shareholders than other, more independent individuals.

## A.4: APPOINTMENTS TO THE BOARD

The Combined Code extends to the recruitment of directors the same principle as has long since been best practice in other recruitment: that there should be a formal, rigorous and transparent procedure for recruiting and appointing new directors to the board. Supporting principles include the sensible suggestion that boards should ensure that potential appointees have enough time to do the role justice, and that there are adequate plans in place for succession to the committee chairman roles.

The recommended recruitment process should be driven by a nomination committee (A.4.1), of which a majority of members should be independent non-executive directors. This committee should be chaired by an independent director, or by the chairman – unless the recruitment exercise is for a successor to the chairman. The terms of reference should be agreed and available, at least on the company's website.[9] The recruitment process should be open and should use either open advertising or a search consultancy (A.4.6).

A job description is a good idea (A.4.2), and the job description for the chairman should take account of the amount of time required by the role; in fact, the time demands are so onerous that the Code recommends that no individual should be appointed simultaneously to a second chairmanship of a FTSE 100 company (A.4.3). Similarly, the Code says that no executive director should have more than one non-executive role in a FTSE 100 company or the chairmanship of such a company (A.4.5).

Non-executive terms of appointment should be available for inspection and should take account of the time requirement, which non-executives should undertake to meet. Other significant involvements should be disclosed (A.4.4).

The Higgs Report, which is within the Combined Code and has advisory status, contains a summary of the principal duties of the nomination committee and a pre-appointment checklist for new board members, as well as a sample letter for appointing a non-executive director. They are all useful and should be reviewed.

# A.5: INFORMATION AND PROFESSIONAL DEVELOPMENT

The main principle here is that 'the board should be supplied in a timely manner with information in a form and of a quality appropriate to enable it to discharge its duties. All directors should receive induction on joining the board and should regularly update and refresh their skills and knowledge.'

The chairman is responsible for ensuring that directors receive timely, accurate and useful information; while management must provide this information, directors are entitled to – and should – seek clarification and amplification wherever they think necessary.

Directors should continually update their skills and knowledge, and the company should provide the resources necessary for this to happen.

The company secretary should be responsible for advising the board on all matters of corporate governance.

The Code requirements are that new directors should receive a full induction when joining the board (A.5.1), that all directors have access to independent legal advice (at the company's expense) where they judge it necessary (A.5.2) and that all directors should have access to the company secretary, whose appointment and removal should be a matter for the board as a whole (A.5.3).

The Higgs Report includes an induction checklist.

# A.6: PERFORMANCE EVALUATION

The Combined Code doesn't see why directors should be immune from performance evaluation, and the main principle is that 'the board should undertake a formal and rigorous annual evaluation of its own performance and that of its committees and individual directors'. This has only one supporting principle (A.6.1), which is that the company's annual report should describe how performance evaluation of the board, its committees and its individual directors has been carried out. Even the chairman is subject to review, and this should be led by the senior independent director with support from the other non-executive and executive directors.

The Higgs Report includes a performance evaluation checklist.

# A.7: RE-ELECTION

The Code's recommendation reflects the requirements of the Companies Act 2006: all directors should be submitted for re-election at regular intervals, subject to continued satisfactory performance. The board, in addition, should ensure planned and progressive refreshing of the board, encouraging those who have become less independent or 'too long in the tooth' to make way for different views and perspectives, remembering always the need (particularly in smaller boards) to ensure that the corporate memory is retained.

The Code says that all directors should be subject to re-election by the shareholders at the annual general meeting immediately following their election (A.7.1) and at three-yearly intervals thereafter. Shareholders should be provided with sufficient information, including that gained through performance reviews, to make an informed decision. Non-executives should only rarely serve more than two three-year terms, and then only after rigorous examination (A.7.2); after three terms, their independence is no longer evident.

# NOTES

1.  Note that the Companies Act does not recognize a specific role for the board; it recognizes that directors have meetings and that decisions are made at those meetings, but is consistently clear that the directors are accountable, both jointly and severally, for those decisions.
2.  Note that the *QCA Corporate Governance Guidelines for AIM Companies* does not include this recommendation.
3.  The Combined Code on Corporate Governance 2006, A.3.1.
4.  The *QCA Guidance for Smaller Quoted Companies* recognizes that there might be only two non-executive directors, one of whom might be the chairman.
5.  The 2006 version of the Combined Code amended the earlier restriction on the chairman serving on the remuneration committee, provided that he or she met the independence criteria on appointment as chairman. In smaller and AIM companies, the QCA argues that it will be essential for the chairman to serve on the remuneration committee (as on the other two) and allows for the possibility that the chairman might also chair an AIM company's remuneration committee.
6.  The *QCA Corporate Governance Guidelines for AIM Companies* contains, at Appendix B, a list of factors that might be taken to impair a non-executive's independence.
7.  While this position is adopted by the Combined Code, the QCA continues to recommend that smaller companies should be able to continue treating the chairman as independent for so long as he or she continues to meet all the tests of independence other than being chairman.
8.  Only in FTSE 350 companies.
9.  A set of model terms of reference for the nomination committee is included in Appendix 5.

# The company secretary

The company secretary has a key corporate governance role to play. The statutory basis of the company secretary's role has evolved over many years and is now contained within the Companies Act 2006.

## COMPANY SECRETARY – STATUTORY FRAMEWORK

The statutory framework for the company secretary's role is contained in Chapter 12 of the Companies Act 2006, sections 270 to 280. While private companies are no longer required to have a company secretary (section 270), it is mandatory for a public (not just a quoted) company to have one (section 271). The directors have to take 'all reasonable steps' to ensure that the company secretary is appropriately qualified, which means that the company secretary must be someone who:

(1)  (a)  is a person who appears to them to have the requisite knowledge and experience to discharge the functions of secretary of the company, and

     (b)  has one or more of the following qualifications.

(2)  The qualifications are –

     (a)  that he has held the office of secretary of a public company for at least three of the five years immediately preceding his appointment as secretary;

     (b)  that he is a member of any of the bodies specified in subsection (3);

(c)   that he is a barrister, advocate or solicitor called or admitted in any part of the United Kingdom;

(d)   that he is a person who, by virtue of his holding or having held any other position or his being a member of any other body, appears to the directors to be capable of discharging the functions of secretary of the company.

(3)   The bodies referred to in subsection (2) (b) are –

(a)   the Institute of Chartered Accountants in England and Wales;

(b)   the Institute of Chartered Accountants of Scotland;

(c)   the Association of Chartered Certified Accountants;

(d)   the Institute of Chartered Accountants in Ireland;

(e)   the Institute of Chartered Secretaries and Administrators;

(f)   the Chartered Institute of Management Accountants;

(g)   the Chartered Institute of Public Finance and Accountancy.[1]

The company secretary is not a director of the company. This is not to say the directors cannot appoint someone to be both director and secretary but, if they do so, such a person cannot act in a dual capacity in respect of something that must be approved by both a director and the secretary (section 280).

The Institute of Chartered Secretaries and Administrators (ICSA) issued a guidance note in 2002 that described the role of the company secretary:[2]

■   Ensuring the smooth running of the board's and board committees' activities by helping the Chairman to set agendas, preparing papers and presenting papers to the board and board committees, advising on board procedures and ensuring the board follows them.

■   Keeping under close review all legislative, regulatory and corporate governance developments that might affect the company's operations, and ensuring the board is fully briefed on these and that it has regard to them when taking decisions.

■   Ensuring that the concept of stakeholders (particularly employees – see section 309 Companies Act 1985) is in the board's mind when important business decisions are being taken. Keeping in touch with the debate on Corporate Social Responsibility and stakeholders, and monitoring all developments in this area and advising the board in relation to its policy and practices with regard to Corporate Social Responsibility and its reporting on that matter.

▌ To act as a confidential sounding board to the Chairman, non-executive directors and executive directors on points that may concern them, and to take a lead role in managing difficult inter-personal issues on the board eg the exit of the directors from the business.

▌ To act as a primary point of contact and source of advice and guidance for, particularly, non-executive directors as regards the company and its activities in order to support the decision making process.

▌ To act as an additional enquiring voice in relation to board decisions which particularly affect the company, drawing on his experience and knowledge of the practical aspects of management including law, tax and business finance. To act as the 'conscience of the company'.

▌ To ensure, where applicable, that the standards and/or disclosures required by the Combined Code annexed to the UK Listing Rules are observed and, where required, reflected in the annual report of the directors – the secretary usually takes the lead role in drafting the annual report, including the Remuneration disclosures and agreeing these with the board and board committee.

▌ Compliance with the continuing obligations of the Listing Rules eg ensuring publications and dissemination of Report and Accounts and interim reports within the periods laid down in the Listing Rules; dissemination of Regulatory News Announcements such as Trading Statements to the market; ensuring that proper notification is made of directors' dealings and the acquisition of interests in the company's incentive arrangements.

▌ Managing relations with investors, particularly institutional investors, with regard to corporate governance issues and the board's practices in relation to corporate governance.

▌ To induct new directors into the business and their roles and responsibilities.

▌ As regards offences under the Financial Services and Markets Act (eg s395), ensuring that the board is fully aware of its responsibility to ensure that it does not mislead the market by putting out or allowing the release of misleading information about its financial performance or trading condition, or by omitting to state information which it should state, or by engaging in a course of conduct which could amount to misleading the market.

▌ Ensuring compliance with all statutory filings, eg forms 288, 88(2), Annual Returns, filing of resolutions adopted at Annual General Meetings/new Articles of Association and any other filings required to be made with Companies House.

▌ Making arrangements for and managing the whole process of the Annual General Meeting and establishing, with the board's agreement, the items to be considered at the AGM, including resolutions dealing with governance type matters, eg the vote on the Remuneration Report and votes on special incentive schemes involving directors. Information about proxy votes etc.

# NOTES

1.  Companies Act 2006, section 273.
2.  'The information given in this Guidance Note, is provided in good faith with the intention of furthering the understanding of the subject matter. Whilst we believe the information to be accurate at the time of publication, ICSA and its staff cannot however accept any liability for any loss or damage occasioned by any person or organisation acting or refraining from action as a result of any views expressed therein. If the reader has any specific doubts or concerns about the subject matter they are advised to seek legal advice based on the circumstances of their own situation.' © Institute of Chartered Secretaries and Administrators, 16 Park Crescent, London W1B 1AH (tel: 020 7580 4741; fax: 020 7323 1132).

# 10

# Directors' remuneration

Directors' remuneration is, in the United Kingdom, a far more vexed issue than, for instance, it appears to be in the United States. The term 'remuneration' includes service contracts as well as financial and non-financial compensation and incentives. Directors' remuneration is right at the heart of corporate governance and is also a central battleground between the stewardship and agency theories of corporate governance. In the UK, the debate has been fairly conclusively settled in favour of the agency theory. As a result, both the statutory and the non-statutory frameworks within which directors' remuneration is settled have become extremely prescriptive. It is an issue that concerns directors as well as corporate governance practitioners and, therefore, I deal with it here at some length.

## DIRECTORS' REMUNERATION – STATUTORY FRAMEWORK

One of the first issues that vexes shareholders, regulators and the press is the length of directors' contracts. Where directors are able to award themselves long-term service contracts, with onerous termination provisions, it will be difficult and expensive for the company to terminate underperforming directors. It has been an area of significant abuse over the last decade.

The Companies Act 2006 therefore has specific requirements in terms of the approval that must be given to contracts that are longer than two years:

**188 Directors' long-term service contracts: requirement of members' approval**

(1)   This section applies to provision under which the guaranteed term of a director's employment –

(a)   with the company of which he is a director, or

(b)   where he is the director of a holding company, within the group consisting of that company and its subsidiaries,

is, or may be, longer than two years.

(2)   A company may not agree to such provision unless it has been approved –

(a)   by resolution of the members of the company, and

(b)   in the case of a director of a holding company, by resolution of the members of that company.

(3)   The guaranteed term of a director's employment is –

(a)   the period (if any) during which the director's employment –

(i)   is to continue, or may be continued otherwise than at the instance of the company (whether under the original agreement or under a new agreement entered into in pursuance of it), and

(ii)   cannot be terminated by the company by notice, or can be so terminated only in specified circumstances, or

(b)   in the case of employment terminable by the company by notice, the period of notice required to be given, or, in the case of employment having a period within paragraph (a) and a period within paragraph (b), the aggregate of those periods.

(4)   If more than six months before the end of the guaranteed term of a director's employment the company enters into a further service contract (otherwise than in pursuance of a right conferred, by or under the original contract, on the other party to it), this section applies as if there were added to the guaranteed term of the new contract the unexpired period of the guaranteed term of the original contract.

Section 189 goes on to say that any contract agreed in contravention of section 188 is automatically void (to the extent of the contravention) and is deemed to contain a clause entitling the company to terminate it at will by giving reasonable notice.

Sections 215 and 216 cover payments for loss of office and reflect that these payments could be made up in a number of ways (including non-cash benefits) and relate to a number of different ways in which the loss of office has come about. Unless the payment is to discharge an existing legal obligation, or to compensate for the breach of such an obligation (section 220), such payments must (unless the company is a subsidiary of another) be approved by a resolution of the members (section 221). Penalties in this section include personal liability to rectify on those directors who authorize payments in contravention of the law.

Sections 227 to 299 of the Companies Act 2006 set out the requirements in relation to retention and availability of, and publicity for, directors' service contracts.

## The Directors' Remuneration Report Regulations 2002[1]

Remuneration, particularly in public companies, is even more contentious and complex than is the issue of service contracts. All companies are required to disclose a substantial amount of information about directors' remuneration by way of notes to their annual accounts. These requirements are waived for quoted companies; instead, they are now legally required to prepare a directors' remuneration report for each financial year, which must be approved by and signed on behalf of the directors and which is subject to external audit. Failure to prepare such a report renders the directors individually liable to financial sanction. The report must be approved by the members of the company in general meeting.

The Directors' Remuneration Report Regulations are a statutory instrument that amended sections of the Companies Act 1985. The Regulations will be replaced by sections 420 to 422 of the Companies Act 2006 as the Act is implemented; Schedule 7A of the Directors' Remuneration Report Regulations 2002 will, however, continue to provide the detail as to what must be contained in the remuneration report. They specifically only apply to quoted companies, not to public or private companies; a quoted company is defined 'as a company whose equity share capital has been included in the official list in accordance with the provisions of Part VI of the Financial Services and Markets Act 2000, is officially listed in an EEA State or is admitted to dealing on either the New York Stock Exchange or the exchange known as Nasdaq'.[2] AIM listed companies are not members of the Official List.

*Quoted companies: directors' remuneration report*[3]

### 234B Duty to prepare directors' remuneration report

(1) The directors of a quoted company shall for each financial year prepare a directors' remuneration report which shall contain the information specified in Schedule 7A and comply with any requirement of that Schedule as to how information is to be set out in the report.

Clause 7 of these regulations inserts a new section 241A into the Companies Act 1985, which requires that a resolution approving the directors' remuneration report for the financial year is moved as an ordinary resolution at the general meeting of the company before which the company's annual accounts for the financial year are laid.

A quoted company is, in addition, required to file a copy of the directors' remuneration report with the Registrar of Companies.

Part 2 of Schedule 7A requires the provision of information on four topics:

1.  Information as to which directors were members of any remuneration committee that dealt with directors' remuneration during the year, information about any person who provided that committee with advice, and details of any other services provided to the company by that person.

2.  A statement of the company's policy on directors' remuneration for the following financial year, and years subsequent to that.

3.  A performance graph that sets out the total shareholder return of the company on the class of equity share capital, if any, that caused the company to fall within the definition of 'quoted company'.

4.  Finally, Part 2 requires provision of specific details in respect of each director's contract of service or contract for services, including details of notice periods, provisions for compensation on loss of office, and so on.

Part 3 of Schedule 7A requires detailed information to be reported concerning the emoluments, share options, long-term incentive plans, pensions, compensation and excess retirement benefits of each director and, in some cases, of past directors as well.

The information required by Schedule 7A is extensive and detailed, and directors need to ensure that their remuneration decisions can be adequately described as required by the regulations. The schedule itself is set out in Appendix 6, and directors – particularly members of remuneration committees – should familiarize themselves with its contents.

# DIRECTORS' REMUNERATION – NON-STATUTORY FRAMEWORK

The non-statutory UK framework for dealing with directors' remuneration in public companies is contained in the Listing Rules and in Section B of the Combined Code on Corporate Governance.

## Listing Rules

The UKLA Listing Rules contain specific requirements (set out in LR 9.8.8 and reproduced below) in respect of reporting on directors' remuneration. The directors' report to the shareholders must (where relevant, in addition to the requirements of the Directors' Remuneration Report Regulations) contain the following:

(1)    a statement of the listed company's policy on executive directors' remuneration;

(2)    information presented in tabular form, unless inappropriate, together with explanatory notes as necessary on:

    (a)    the amount of each element in the remuneration package for the period under review of each director, by name, including, but not restricted to, basic salary and fees, the estimated money value of benefits in kind, annual bonuses, deferred bonuses, compensation for loss of office and payments for breach of contract or other termination payments;

    (b)    the total remuneration for each director for the period under review and for the corresponding prior period;

    (c)    any significant payments made to former directors during the period under review; and

    (d)    any share options, including Save-as-you-earn options, for each director, by name, in accordance with the requirements of the Directors' Remuneration Report Regulations;

(3)   details of any long-term incentive schemes, other than share options as required by paragraph (2)(d), including the interests of each director, by name, in the long-term incentive schemes at the start of the period under review;

(4)   details of any entitlements or awards granted and commitments made to each director under any long-term incentive schemes during the period, showing which crystallise either in the same year or in subsequent years;

(5)   details of the monetary value and number of shares, cash payments or other benefits received by each director under any long-term incentive schemes during the period;

(6)   details of the interests of each director in the long-term incentive schemes at the end of the period;

(7)   an explanation and justification of any element of a director's remuneration, other than basic salary, which is pensionable;

(8)   details of any directors' service contract with a notice period in excess of one year or with provisions for pre-determined compensation on termination which exceeds one year's salary and benefits in kind, giving the reasons for such notice period;

(9)   details of the unexpired term of any directors' service contract of a director proposed for election or re-election at the forthcoming annual general meeting, and, if any director proposed for election or re-election does not have a directors' service contract, a statement to that effect;

(10)   a statement of the listed company's policy on the granting of options or awards under its employees' share schemes and other long-term incentive schemes, explaining and justifying any departure from that policy in the period under review and any change in the policy from the preceding year;

(11)   for money purchase schemes details of the contribution or allowance payable or made by the listed company in respect of each director during the period under review; and

(12)   for defined benefit schemes:

(a)   details of the amount of the increase during the period under review (excluding inflation) and of the accumulated total amount at the end of the period in respect of the accrued benefit to which each director would be entitled on leaving service or is entitled having left service during the period under review;

(b) either:

   (i) the transfer value (less director's contributions) of the relevant increase in accrued benefit (to be calculated in accordance with Actuarial Guidance Note GN11 but making no deduction for any under-funding) as at the end of the period; or

   (ii) so much of the following information as is necessary to make a reasonable assessment of the transfer value in respect of each director:

      (A) age;

      (B) normal retirement age;

      (C) the amount of any contributions paid or payable by the director under the terms of the scheme during the period under review;

      (D) details of spouse's and dependants' benefits;

      (E) early retirement rights and options;

      (F) expectations of pension increases after retirement (whether guaranteed or discretionary); and

      (G) discretionary benefits for which allowance is made in transfer values on leaving and any other relevant information which will significantly affect the value of the benefits; and

(c) no disclosure of voluntary contributions and benefits.

It is logical that there should be only one directors' remuneration report contained in the annual accounts and that it should contain all the information necessary to comply with both the Listing Rules and the Companies Act 2006.

## Directors' remuneration and the Combined Code

First, the main principle (B.2) is that there should be a 'formal and transparent procedure for developing policy on executive remuneration and for fixing the remuneration packages of individual directors. No director should be involved in deciding his or her own remuneration.'[4]

The supporting principles are that the:

remuneration committee should consult the chairman and/or chief executive about their proposals relating to the remuneration of other executive directors. The remuneration committee should also be responsible for appointing any consultants in respect of executive director remuneration. Where executive directors or senior management are involved in advising or supporting the remuneration committee, care should be taken to recognise and avoid conflicts of interest.

The chairman of the board should ensure that the company maintains contact as required with its principal shareholders about remuneration in the same way as for other matters.[5]

The Combined Code provides detailed guidance on how these principles should be achieved. There should be a remuneration committee (B.2.1), which should consist of three (two in smaller companies) *independent* non-executive directors. It should have formal terms of reference,[6] which should be available on the company's website, and where remuneration consultants are retained, any other work they do for the company should be made public. The remuneration committee should have delegated authority (B.2.2) to set remuneration terms (including pension, incentive payments, share options, etc) for the executive directors and for the chairman, and to recommend and monitor compensation for the level of management immediately below the board. Where the chairman is a member of the remuneration committee, his or her compensation should be agreed by the board as a whole, as should that of the non-executive directors (B.2.3), and long-term share incentive schemes should be approved by the shareholders (B.2.4).

The Combined Code provides guidance on remuneration as well, and this guidance is in addition to the requirements of the Companies Act 2006, the Listing Rules and the Directors' Remuneration Report Regulations 2002. The main principle (B.1) on the level and make-up of directors' remuneration is that 'levels of remuneration should be sufficient to attract, retain and motivate directors of the quality required to run the company successfully, but a company should avoid paying more than is necessary for this purpose. A significant proportion of executive directors' remuneration should be structured so as to link rewards to corporate and individual performance.'

The Combined Code focuses its remuneration guidance on the performance-related elements of a director's package, which, it says (B.1.1), should form a 'significant proportion of the total remuneration package of executive directors and should be designed to align their interests with those of shareholders and to give these directors keen incentives to perform at the highest levels'. The Combined Code's Schedule A provides specific guidance on the make-up of performance-related pay, and the key principles it stresses are the need for performance requirements to be challenging, for rewards not to be excessive, for share option vesting periods to be at least three years and for directors to be encouraged to hold such shares for at least a further three years. Executive share options should not be granted at a discount (B.1.2) and, although the Combined Code doesn't say this, they should obviously not be backdated to a point in the past at which they would have been more attractively priced.[7]

B.1.3 deals with remuneration for non-executive directors, which the Combined Code says should be proportionate to the time, responsibilities and effort required for the role, and should not include share options (unless, exceptionally, these have first been approved by the shareholders); a non-executive holding of share options is likely to prejudice his or her independence. B.1.4 suggests that, where an executive director is serving elsewhere as a non-executive, compensation for that role should not usually be taken by the director but rather by the company that provides his or her executive employment; in any case, the report should include a statement on how this is dealt with.

Finally, clauses B.1.5 and B.1.6 deal with service contracts, recommending that early termination provisions should be designed, in directors' service contracts, to ensure that directors are not rewarded for poor performance,[8] that there should be a robust approach to requiring departing directors to mitigate their loss and that, in any case, notice periods should not be longer than one year.

# NOTES

1. http://www.opsi.gov.uk/SI/si2002/20021986.htm.
2. Regulation 10 of the Companies Act 1985.
3. This excerpt, and all others in this chapter, are from the Directors' Remuneration Report Regulations 2002, and are Crown Copyright.
4. Combined Code on Corporate Governance, B.2.
5. Ibid.

6.   The ICSA model terms of reference for remuneration committees are included at Appendix 5.

7.   It should be noted that there are specific accounting rules covering share options. IFRS 2, which was issued in February 2004, applies to annual accounting periods beginning on or after 1 January 2005. It applies to grants of shares, share options or other equity instruments made after 7 November 2002 that had not yet been vested at the effective date of the IFRS. It applies retrospectively to liabilities arising from share-based payments that existed at the IFRS effective date. Companies that do issue shares as part of their remuneration package will need to take professional advice to ensure that these grants are correctly accounted for.

8.   The Combined Code footnote to this whole section ('Views have been sought by the Department of Trade and Industry by 30 September 2003 on whether, and if so how, further measures are required to enable shareholders to ensure that compensation reflects performance when directors' contracts are terminated: See "Rewards for Failure": Directors' Remuneration – Contracts, performance and severance, June 2003') is a warning that, unless companies do take robust steps to ensure that poor performance by directors is not rewarded, legislation can be expected to take up the slack.

# 11

# The Combined Code and financial reporting

Section C.1 of the Combined Code deals with financial reporting. The main principle is that the board should present a balanced and understandable assessment of the company's position and prospects. The supporting principle is that the board's responsibility to present a balanced and understandable assessment extends to interim and other price-sensitive public reports and reports to regulators as well as to information required to be presented by statutory requirements.

It should be noted that the Listing Rules require the company's auditors to review and report on the company's compliance with this principle; there is a parallel here to the SOX requirements on auditor review of executive attestation.

## THE STATUTORY FRAMEWORK FOR FINANCIAL REPORTING

Part 15 of the Companies Act 2006 sets out the statutory framework within which UK companies must keep financial records. Section 386, 'Duty to keep accounting records', says:

Every company must keep adequate accounting records.
Adequate accounting records means records that are sufficient –

(a)    to show and explain the company's transactions,

(b)    to disclose with reasonable accuracy, at any time, the financial position of the company at that time, and

(c)   to enable the directors to ensure that any accounts required to be prepared comply with the requirements of
this Act (and, where applicable, of Article 4 of the IAS
Regulation).

(3)   Accounting records must, in particular, contain –

(a)   entries from day to day of all sums of money received
and expended by the company and the matters in respect
of which the receipt and expenditure takes place, and

(b)   a record of the assets and liabilities of the company.

Directors are explicitly responsible for producing the company's accounts
(section 394: 'the directors of every company must prepare accounts for
the company for each of its financial years').

These records are, in accordance with section 396, summarized in a
company's profit and loss account (the P&L, sometimes called a trading
statement) and its balance sheet. The P&L is a summary of activity that
has taken place over a defined period of time; the balance sheet is a
snapshot of the assets and liabilities of the organization at a particular
point in time. Section 396 requires these accounts to give a 'true and fair
view'. In the case of the balance sheet, it must give a true and fair view of
the state of affairs of the company as at the end of the financial year, and
in the case of the profit and loss account, it must give a true and fair view
of the profit or loss of the company for the financial year. Consolidated
group accounts must, similarly, give a true and fair view of the group's
balance sheet and profit or loss. The Companies Act also sets out what
sort of information must be provided on each of a number of subjects,
including directors' remuneration and employee details.

Finally, the annual accounts must be approved by the directors and
the balance sheet signed on behalf of the board by one of the directors
(section 414).

Directors are jointly and severally guilty of an offence if they fail to
keep proper accounting records, and these records must be retained, in
the case of a public company, for a period of six years from the date they
were made.

The Code Provisions are:

C.1.1   The directors should explain in the annual report their
responsibility for preparing the accounts and there should
be a statement by the auditors about their reporting responsibilities, and

C.1.2 The directors should report that the business is a going concern, with supporting assumptions or qualifications as necessary.

It should be noted that it is a requirement of the Listing Rules (LR 9.8.10) that the company's auditors review both the directors' statement that the company is a going concern and the statement in C.1.1 above.

# ACCOUNTING STANDARDS

Accounts are prepared in accordance with the requirements of the Companies Act 2006 (Part 15) and with generally accepted accounting standards. Accounting standards are, on their own, a substantial area of professional knowledge; the corporate governance practitioner needs to be aware of the overall direction of debate and development in this area, and able to draw on appropriate professional advice, as there are significant impacts on organizations resulting from how they choose to report.

Prior to 2005, all UK companies were required by the Companies Act 1985 to adopt UK Generally Accepted Accounting Principles (UK GAAP) in the preparation of their accounts. From January 2005, UK companies were allowed to use International Accounting Standards in their individual accounts as an alternative to UK accounting standards; this gave effect to the EU regulation requirement that listed companies use IAS when preparing consolidated accounts.

On 1 April 2001, the International Accounting Standards Board (IASB) assumed accounting standard-setting responsibilities from its predecessor body, the International Accounting Standards Committee. The IASB is a privately funded organization (with charitable status) committed:

> to developing, in the public interest, a single set of high quality, understandable and enforceable global accounting standards [the International Financial Reporting Standards, or IFRS, sometimes referred to as International Accounting Standards, or IAS] that require transparent and comparable information in general purpose financial statements. In addition, the IASB co-operates with national accounting standard-setters to achieve convergence in accounting standards around the world.[1]

Before standards as written by the IASB can be used by UK companies they are required to be adopted in the European Union. The Accounting

Regulatory Committee (ARC) is composed of representatives from member states and chaired by the Commission. The function of the Committee is a regulatory one and consists of providing an opinion on Commission proposals to adopt (endorse) an international accounting standard.

The vast majority of entities in the UK, however, continue to use UK GAAP, and a new and revised edition of this was released in 2007. The UK Accounting Standards Board, which is responsible for UK GAAP, believes that it is pointless for the UK to have two parallel accounting standards and has a strategy of converging UK GAAP with IAS, which involves a step-by-step replacement of existing UK standards with IAS ones.

# AUDITOR'S REPORT

The auditor reports to the members of the company (not to the directors) and is required to state (under section 495) whether, in his or her opinion, the annual accounts:

(a)   give a true and fair view

  (i)   in the case of an individual balance sheet, of the state of affairs of the company as at the end of the financial year,

  (ii)   in the case of an individual profit and loss account, of the profit or loss of the company for the financial year,

  (iii)   in the case of group accounts, of the state of affairs as at the end of the financial year and of the profit or loss for the financial year of the undertakings included in the consolidation as a whole, so far as concerns members of the company;

(b)   have been properly prepared in accordance with the relevant financial reporting framework; and

(c)   have been prepared in accordance with the requirements of [the Companies Act 2006] (and, where applicable, Article 4 of the IAS Regulation).

Auditors who issue audit reports that 'include any matter that is misleading, false, deceptive in a material particular' (section 507), or omit any statements required by the Act, will be guilty of an offence.

# AUDIT QUALIFICATIONS

Section 496 says the auditor's report:

(a) must be either unqualified or qualified, and

(b) must include a reference to any matters to which the auditor wishes to draw attention by way of emphasis without qualifying the report.

All audit firms have strict internal rules about the basis on which they can or will qualify the accounts of an audit client, and because any qualification can have a damaging effect on the creditworthiness of a client and the market value of its shares (not to mention the reputation of its executive officers and, in particular, the finance director), qualifications are not lightly made.

The auditor is also required (section 496) to report on the directors' report (a narrative report that the directors, by law, are required to include in the accounts) and must state 'whether in his opinion the information given in the directors' report for the financial year for which the accounts are prepared is consistent with those accounts'.

Under section 499, auditors have the right to access the company's books and records at all times and may require any person involved with the company to provide them with information and explanations as they think necessary for the performance of their duties. Section 500 extends this right to overseas subsidiaries. Under section 501, anyone who either fails to comply with a requirement to provide information or 'conveys or purports to convey any information or explanations which the auditor requires, or is entitled to require, under section 499, and which is misleading, false or deceptive in a material particular' will be guilty of an offence. In parallel, section 418 (which deals with the directors' report) contains a requirement that the directors' report must contain a statement that each director has ensured that:

(a) so far as the director is aware, there is no relevant audit information of which the company's auditor is unaware, and

(b) he has taken all the steps that he ought to have taken as a director in order to make himself aware of any relevant audit information and to establish that the company's auditor is aware of that information.

(3)   'Relevant audit information' means information needed by the company's auditor in connection with preparing his report.

(4)   A director is regarded as having taken all the steps that he ought to have taken as a director in order to do the things mentioned in subsection (2)(b) if he has –

    (a)   made such enquiries of his fellow directors and of the company's auditors for that purpose, and

    (b)   taken such other steps (if any) for that purpose, as are required by his duty as a director of the company to exercise reasonable care, skill and diligence.

# NOTE

1.   www.iasb.org.

# 12

# Risk management

Risk management has always been a key governance issue. A key issue reserved to the board is the corporate strategy and, therefore, strategic risk has always been a de facto board responsibility. The modern corporation's fundamental goal is to create and add value to its business continuously. The strategic management goal is to find an appropriate balance between profit maximization and risk reduction.

## RISK MANAGEMENT AND CORPORATE GOVERNANCE

The objective of balancing profit maximization against risk reduction was recognized in the UK corporate governance framework. Following the work of the Smith and Higgs committees, the Combined Code on Corporate Governance was revised and reissued in July 2003. The Turnbull Report was renamed the Turnbull Guidance and included in the revised Combined Code.

In Section 1, the revised Combined Code states that the 'board's role is to provide entrepreneurial leadership of the company within a framework of prudent and effective controls which enables risk to be assessed and managed'. Risk management, in other words, had now been identified as a key responsibility for the board. The non-executive directors are required to 'satisfy themselves on the integrity of financial information and that financial controls and systems of risk management are robust and defensible'.

The Companies Act 2006 requires UK companies to publish, as part of their annual report,[1] a business review, which must contain 'to the extent necessary for an understanding of the development, performance or position of the company's business... a description of the principal risks and uncertainties facing the business'.[2] This can only be done properly if the company has in place a risk management framework.

In the last few years, the parallel importance of operational risk ('the risk of direct or indirect loss resulting from inadequate or failed internal processes, people and systems or from external events'[3]) has been recognized. The United Kingdom's Combined Code requires listed companies to review annually 'all material controls, including financial, operational and compliance controls, and risk management systems'.[4]

The Turnbull Guidance explicitly requires boards, *on an ongoing basis*, to identify, assess and deal with significant risks in all areas, including in information and communications processes.[5] The key questions that directors of listed companies are expected to answer (which are not meant to be exhaustive) are set out in Appendix 1 to the Turnbull Guidance and are quoted below. Key questions include:

▪ Are the significant internal and external operational, financial, compliance and other risks identified and assessed on an ongoing basis? (Significant risks may, for example, include those related to market, credit, liquidity, technological, legal, health, safety and environmental, reputation, and business probity issues.)

▪ Does the board have clear strategies for dealing with the significant risks that have been identified? Is there a policy on how to manage these risks?

▪ Are information needs and related information systems reassessed as objectives and related risks change or as reporting deficiencies are identified?

▪ Are there specific arrangements for management monitoring and reporting to the board on risk and control matters of particular importance? These could include, for example, actual or suspected fraud and other illegal or irregular acts, or matters that could adversely affect the company's reputation or financial position.

Sarbanes–Oxley requires US listed companies to assess annually the effectiveness of their internal controls, and places a number of other significant governance burdens on executive officers, including the section 409 requirement that companies notify the SEC 'on a rapid and current basis [of] such additional information concerning material changes in the financial condition or operations of the issuer'.

Risk management is, in other words, an international cornerstone of today's corporate governance framework. In the context of both strategic and operational risk, a risk assessment is the first step that a board can take to controlling its risk; the next important step is the development of a risk treatment plan (in which risks are accepted, controlled, eliminated or contracted out) that is appropriate in the context of the company's strategic business objectives.

The role of risk management and internal control is described clearly in the Turnbull Guidance:

> A company's objectives, its internal organisation and the environment in which it operates are continually evolving and, as a result, the risks it faces are continually changing. A sound system of internal control therefore depends on a thorough and regular evaluation of the nature and extent of the risks to which the company is exposed. Since profits are, in part, the reward for successful risk-taking in business, the purpose of internal control is to help manage and control risk appropriately rather than to eliminate it.[6]

# RISK ASSESSMENT AND RISK MANAGEMENT

Risk assessment and risk management are a common theme of corporate governance and internal control structures. All organizations face risks of one sort or another on a daily basis. Risk management is a discipline for dealing with non-speculative risks, those risks from which only a loss can occur. Speculative risks, those from which either a profit or a loss can occur, are the subject of the organization's business strategy, whereas non-speculative risks, which can reduce the value of the assets with which the organization undertakes its speculative activity, should be the subject of a risk management plan. These non-speculative risks are sometimes called permanent and 'pure' risks, in order to differentiate them from the crisis and speculative types. The identification of a risk as either speculative or permanent will reflect the organization's risk appetite.

Risk management plans generally have four, linked, objectives. These are to:

1.  eliminate risks;

2.   reduce those that can't be eliminated to 'acceptable' levels; and then to either

3.   live with them, exercising carefully the controls that keep them 'acceptable'; or

4.   transfer them, by means of insurance, to some other organization.

Pure, permanent risks are usually identifiable in economic terms; they have a financially measurable potential impact upon the assets of the organization. Risk management strategies are usually therefore based on an assessment of the economic benefits that the organization can derive from an investment in a particular control; in other words, for every control that the organization might implement, the calculation would be that the cost of implementation should be outweighed, preferably significantly, by the economic benefits that derive from, or economic losses that are avoided as a result of, its implementation. The organization should define its criteria for accepting risks (for example, it might say that it will accept any risk whose economic impact is less than the cost of controlling it) and for controlling risks (for example, it might say that any risk that has both a high likelihood and a high impact must be controlled down to an identified level, or threshold).

# RISK ASSESSMENT

A systematic approach to risk assessment should take into account business, legal and regulatory requirements placed on the business. In other words, it must be business-driven. This is one of the most important ideas underlying internal control: the business, managed by its board of directors, should identify the threats to assets, vulnerabilities and impacts on the organization and should determine the degree of risk that it is prepared to accept – in the light of its business model, business strategy and investment criteria. Risk assessment is a 'systematic study of assets, threats, vulnerabilities and impacts to assess the probability and consequences of risks'[7] or, in our terms, the systematic and methodical consideration of: 1) the business harm likely to result from a range of business failures; and 2) the realistic likelihood of such failures occurring.

Qualitative risk analysis has, for a long time, been by far the most widely used approach, although quantitative methodologies – driven by Basel 2 (see page 100) – are on the increase. Risk analysis can be a subjective exercise in any environment where returns are derived from taking risks, unless there is a comprehensive database (as required by Basel 2) of risk events from which likelihoods could be calculated mathematically. Otherwise all individual inputs into the analysis will reflect individual prejudice, and so the process of information gathering should question inputs to establish what really is known – and what unknown.

# CONTROLS

At this granular level, controls are the countermeasures for risks. Apart from knowingly accepting risks that fall within the criteria of acceptability, or transferring the risk (through insurance) to others, there are four types of control:

1.  deterrent controls, which reduce the likelihood of a deliberate attack;

2.  preventative controls, which protect vulnerabilities and make an attack or other event unsuccessful or reduce its impact;

3.  corrective controls, which reduce the effect of an attack or business failure;

4.  detective controls, which discover attacks or other risk events and trigger preventative or corrective controls.

It is essential that any controls that are implemented are cost-effective. The principle is that the cost of implementing and maintaining a control should be no greater than the cost of the impact. It is not cost-effectively possible to provide total protection against every single risk; the trade-off therefore involves providing effective security against most, but not all, risks.

# RISK MANAGEMENT

No organization should invest in risk controls or implement processes and procedures without having carried out an appropriate risk assessment that assures them that:

1.  the proposed investment (the total cost of the control) is the same as or less than the cost of the identified event's impact;

2.    the risk classification takes into account its probability; and

3.    the priority of the risk is appropriate, ie all the risks with higher prioritizations have already been adequately controlled.

If the organization cannot satisfy itself that the proposed investment meets these criteria, it will be wasting money – and the time required to implement the control – while leaving itself open to more likely risks and, conceivably, with inadequate resources to respond to the more likely risk when it occurs. There is, in other words, a risk associated with not doing an adequate risk assessment and maintaining a risk management framework, and directors should carefully consider this risk (and their fiduciary duties) before proceeding without one.

# BIS AND BASEL 2

Banking failure can be more catastrophic than any other failure. Banking organizations are therefore expected to go further in risk management terms than other commercial entities. In the banking world, an international accounting and risk management framework, driven by the Bank of International Settlements (BIS), has already emerged. BIS is the central banks' central bank. It exclusively serves central banks and other international organizations, and its declared aim is to 'foster cooperation among central banks and other agencies in pursuit of monetary and financial stability'.

In June 2004, the Bank's Basel Committee on Banking Supervision published its *International Convergence of Capital Measurement and Capital Standards: A Revised Framework*, which has become known as Basel 2. (Basel 1, the Basel Capital Accord of 1988, set out the first internationally accepted definition of, and measurement for, bank capital. It is thought to have been adopted in more than 100 countries.) The Basel 2 framework detailed 'more risk-sensitive requirements' for banking organizations in assessing their capital adequacy and 'seeks to strengthen market discipline by enhancing transparency in banks' financial reporting'.[8]

While the chairman of the Basel Committee on Banking Supervision has admitted that 'implementing the Basel 2 rules governing international banks' capital will be as difficult and important as drawing up the rules, which took five years', there can be no doubt about BIS's determination to complete the implementation, the start date for which was 2007. While practical difficulties have led to a deferral in the actual start date, the implementation of these rules is now inescapable.

# BASEL 2 AND OPERATIONAL RISK

The financial sector differentiates operational risk from market and credit risk. Operational risk has become a key issue for banks and financial services firms as a direct result of the combined effects of the deregulation of financial services, the globalization of markets, and the growing sophistication of information technology. Operational risk is defined as 'the risk of loss resulting from inadequate or failed internal processes, people and systems, or from external events'.[9]

The Basel Committee excluded legal and reputational risk from its definition of operational risk, on the grounds that these were possible consequences of a failure to manage operational risk effectively. Operational risk categories include risks in processes (eg compliance issues, incorrect asset allocation, mis-pricing, and accounting and taxation errors), risks arising from people (eg unauthorized trading, insider dealing, or employee relations issues such as recruitment, discrimination and termination), systems risks (such as hardware or software failure, issues over availability and integrity of data, and utility failures), and external events (eg terrorist attack, vandalism and supplier failure).

Basel 2 seeks to achieve its goal of strengthening the international financial system through three pillars. Pillar 1 aims to align a bank's minimum capital requirements more closely to its actual risk of economic loss, intending to establish an explicit capital charge for a bank's exposures to operational risk. Those banks whose approaches to measuring, managing and controlling their operational risk exposures are appropriate to the risk area will have lower capital requirements. While Pillar 2 allows for supervisory review of banks' risk management processes, Pillar 3 explicitly sets out to enhance transparency in banks' public reporting in order to 'leverage the ability of market discipline to motivate prudent management'.

While not all financial institutions are enthusiastic about embracing operational risk management methodologies (because, while the impact of operational risk is not always clear, the actual day-to-day cost of implementing an operational risk management approach tends to be very clear, and there's not always equal clarity about the real business value of the implementation), it can only be effective if it is driven by the board and management, integrated into the internal control structure and made part of the overall corporate governance framework.

The board must assign management accountability to someone (the chief risk officer, for instance) who will be adequately resourced to drive the programme forward, and the business line managers need to be 'bought in' to the value of the initiative. They will only be 'bought in', though, if the business objectives of the operational risk management initiative clearly include driving down costs (including the cost of economic capital), reducing the burden of regulatory compliance, and improving operational efficiency and customer service. One immediate benefit that ought to be available to business line managers is a reduction in both market risk and credit risk as a result of the reduction in those operational risks that have an immediate impact on the other two categories (such as, for instance, the market loss that arises from unauthorized trading of specific products, or incorrect market positions arising from incorrect data entry).

A key component of an operational risk framework is a set of business line 'loss databases' that include three years' worth of data relating to 'loss events' in each of the various categories of operational risk. In theory, these databases should enable financial institutions to make statistically meaningful estimates of the likelihood and impact of losses arising from operational risk. Not all financial institutions have historical data that are sufficiently granular to make such estimates. Operational risk management tools are also still at an early stage, and there is still no generally accepted 'best-in-class' set of such tools.

The Basel Committee, however, (in February 2003) published *Sound Practices for the Management and Supervision of Operational Risk*, which is a set of generic guidelines but without a detailed road map for how to develop and implement a sound framework. This recognizes that, while individual banks have to develop operational risk management approaches that are appropriate for their circumstances and culture, the key components of an effective approach will be consistent and will include:

▌ a clear, board-driven operational risk strategy with meaningful review, oversight and monitoring;

▌ a strong internal control and operational risk management culture (which includes clear segregation of duties and clear lines of responsibility);

▌ effective internal reporting; and

▌ meaningful contingency planning.

The paper identified 10 principles of 'sound practice', and these included the development of policies, processes and procedures that would implement the board's strategy; effective communication up and down the organization; identification and quantification of risks in all current activities, processes, systems and new products; systems for monitoring operational risk exposures; cost/benefit analysed polices, processes and procedures for controlling or mitigating operational risk; and independent evaluation and reporting on these various systems, processes and procedures.

There are significant similarities and overlap between the operational risk management requirements of Basel 2 and the requirements of the Combined Code, Sarbanes–Oxley and other regulatory and governance frameworks around the world. Boards have to address their risk management responsibilities in a coherent fashion; in other words, they need to develop a single, comprehensive and effective risk management framework that will enable them to meet all their fiduciary obligations while also complying with the whole range of statutory and regulatory risk management requirements that apply to their business.

## ERM FRAMEWORK

Enterprise risk management (ERM) has emerged over the last few years as a fundamentally new way for organizations to approach risk. This is driven partly by the extensive overlap between the risk management requirements of SOX, Turnbull and Basel 2, as well as ongoing changes in the global information economy. Organizations face new and complex risks in a rapidly changing business, technological and regulatory environment. They cannot afford not to identify and control against all areas of risk – including those that might remain unidentified or unforeseen, including currency fluctuations, human resource issues in foreign countries, changing or disappearing distribution channels, corporate governance and regulatory pressures, and the range of risks associated with technology, information and intellectual assets.

## COSO ERM FRAMEWORK

COSO, whose internal control framework[10] has become the de facto standard approach to internal control for US companies complying with SOX,[11] started work on developing a separate risk management framework in 2001. This framework, the *Enterprise Risk Management – Integrated Framework*,[12] was designed to provide a common framework, 'key principles and concepts, a common language, and clear direction and guidance'.[13] This framework expands on the earlier COSO internal control framework, providing a broader and more robust focus on enterprise risk management. Because it incorporates the internal control framework, organizations could (as COSO suggests) move towards implementing an ERM framework to satisfy their internal control needs as well as their broader business risk management needs.

COSO defines ERM as 'a process, effected by an entity's board of directors, management and other personnel, applied in strategy setting and across the enterprise, designed to identify potential events that may affect the entity, and manage risk to be within its risk appetite, to provide reasonable assurance regarding the achievement of entity objectives'. It's a definition broad enough to encompass the Basel 2 definition of operational risk as well as those in Turnbull and SOX. It is absolutely about achieving the organization's business strategy, and it deals with strategic, operational, reporting and compliance goals or objectives.

The COSO ERM framework has eight components:

▌ internal environment;

▌ objective setting;

▌ event identification;

▌ risk assessment;

▌ risk response;

▌ control activities;

▌ information and communication;

▌ monitoring.

An effective ERM framework will be one in which all eight components identified above are present and functioning effectively in each of the four categories of objectives. Of course, the components will not function identically in every organization, and implementations will be less formal and structured in smaller organizations than in larger ones. The COSO ERM framework comes with detailed implementation guidance, and any organization considering adoption, sensibly, of such a framework should acquire and study both the ERM framework and the 'Application techniques', where there are also a number of important general points.

ERM involves analysis and treatment of all business risks – those that are transferable/insurable as well as a wide array of traditionally non-insurable risks. The ERM implementation process is an inherently collaborative one that requires teamwork among many disciplines within an organization. Depending on the business sector, it will require, for instance, risk management, credit management, treasury, and accounting input, as well as operational management, marketing, R&D and the legal department. It is best to have someone specifically charged with leading the ERM process, and this person should have the full support of the CEO, the board and the management.

An organization's ERM framework should, in other words, explicitly include all other risk management frameworks (including, for instance, health and safety) within the organization, and it should deal with all risks, to all assets and to all aspects of the business. It should map each risk to all those assets it might threaten or vulnerabilities it might exploit. It should be built on an explicit and detailed mapping of all the statutory and regulatory compliance requirements faced by the organization, across all the jurisdictions in which it does business or has operations, and should affect all business lines and business activities. There should be a standard enterprise-wide approach to risk assessment, risk classification and risk control, and this should be applied in all activities, from information security through to operational risk management.

At the end of the exercise, the organization's management frameworks need to be integrated and to contribute seamlessly to the organization's achievement of its strategic goals.

## NOTES

1. See further discussion on this report in Chapter 16.
2. Companies Act 2006, section 417.
3. 'Operational risk', a consultative document from the Basel Committee on Banking Supervision in January 2001.
4. Combined Code on Corporate Governance, Section C.2.1, July 2003.
5. Turnbull Guidance, clause 20.
6. Turnbull Guidance, clause 4.
7. ISO 17799:2005.
8. BIS press release, 26 June 2004.
9. BIS press release, 26 June 2004.
10. *Internal Control – Integrated Framework*, first published in September 1992 and further discussed in Chapter 13.
11. It should also be noted that the SEC has formally accepted that the Turnbull Guidance is an acceptable framework for internal control for SOX section 404 compliance purposes.

12. http://www.coso.org/Publications/ERM/COSO_ERM_Executive Summary.pdf.
13. COSO (2004) *Enterprise Risk Management – Integrated Framework*, Executive summary, September, COSO, New York.

# Internal control and the Turnbull Guidance

'A company's system of internal control has a key role in the management of risks that are significant to the fulfilment of its business objectives. A sound system of internal control contributes to safeguarding the shareholders' investment and the company's assets.'[1] Turnbull also identifies clearly the link between risk management and internal control, and sets out the key responsibilities in relation to internal control:

16. The board of directors is responsible for the company's system of internal control. It should set appropriate policies on internal control and seek regular assurance that will enable it to satisfy itself that the system is functioning effectively. The board must further ensure that the system of internal control is effective in managing risks in the manner which it has approved.

17. In determining its policies with regard to internal control, and thereby assessing what constitutes a sound system of internal control in the particular circumstances of the company, the board's deliberations should include consideration of the following factors:

    – the nature and extent of the risks facing the company;

    – the extent and categories of risk which it regards as acceptable for the company to bear;

    – the likelihood of the risks concerned materialising;

  - the company's ability to reduce the incidence and impact on the business of risks that do materialise; and

  - the costs of operating particular controls relative to the benefit thereby obtained in managing the related risks.

18.  It is the role of management to implement board policies on risk and control. In fulfilling its responsibilities, management should identify and evaluate the risks faced by the company for consideration by the board and design, operate and monitor a suitable system of internal control which implements the policies adopted by the board.[2]

Controls, in simple terms, and as we said in the previous chapter, are countermeasures for risks. Internal control frameworks have traditionally been designed to deal primarily with financial risk: the risk that errors or dishonesty could lead to loss of money. From a corporate governance perspective, internal controls must respond to the much wider range of risks identified within the ERM framework discussed in the previous chapter. UK-based companies will look primarily to the Turnbull Guidance on internal control, and the work done on internal control frameworks by the international Treadway Commission, and the US Public Company Accounting Oversight Board (PCAOB)[3] is also, because of its widespread impact, a key reference point for this subject.

# INTERNAL CONTROLS AND AUDIT

Section 302 of the Sarbanes–Oxley Act of 2002 required the management of US listed companies to certify the company's financial reports, and under section 404 the company's independent auditors are required to attest management's certification of the organization's internal controls.[4]

Financial reporting depends critically on the IT infrastructure, whether it is for the rendering of an invoice, the effective operation of an enterprise resource planning (ERP) system, or an integrated, organization-wide management information and control system. Unless appropriate internal controls are built into this infrastructure, management will not be able to make the required certification.

As has already been described, the US Securities and Exchange Commission (the SEC) mandated US companies to use a recognized internal control framework that had been developed through a due process, including inviting public comment. The Turnbull Guidance has been recognized as one such framework. Another widely used framework within North America is known as the COSO framework or, to give it its own title, the *Internal Control – Integrated Framework*, which contains the recommendations of the Committee of Sponsoring Organizations of the Treadway Commission.[5]

# COSO

COSO defines internal control broadly:

> as a process, effected by an entity's board of directors, management and other personnel, designed to provide reasonable assurance regarding the achievement of objectives in the following categories:

▌ Effectiveness and efficiency of operations.

▌ Reliability of financial reporting.

▌ Compliance with applicable laws and regulations.

> The first category addresses an entity's basic business objectives, including performance and profitability goals and safeguarding of resources. The second relates to the preparation of reliable published financial statements, including interim and condensed financial statements and selected financial data derived from such statements, such as earnings releases, reported publicly. The third deals with complying with those laws and regulations to which the entity is subject.[6]

The definition is a good one.

COSO says, and most accounting organizations would agree, that internal control consists of five interrelated elements. These are:

▌ The control environment – the foundation for all other elements, influencing the control consciousness of the people within the organization, and encompassing every aspect of how the organization is structured and works, from the attention and direction provided by the board through to the ethical values and competence of the staff.

▌ Risk assessment – the identification and analysis of risks to the achievement of the organization's business objectives.

▌ Control activities – these are the policies and procedures that help the organization's board and management ensure that their control decisions are carried out in relation to identified risks; they occur at all levels and in all parts of the organization and include, for instance, authorizations, reviews, duty segregation, reconciliations, etc.

▌ Information and communication – must occur at two levels: the board communicates its control objectives clearly to staff throughout the organization (as well as with external parties, and for staff to be able to communicate effectively with management), and the organization's information systems must capture and report pertinent information (operational, financial and compliance-related information as well as external activities and conditions that affect the business) in a time frame and format that enable the organization's board and management to carry out their responsibilities.

▌ Monitoring – the ongoing monitoring of internal control systems includes regular and ad hoc functional and management reviews, and should be based on a risk assessment, with serious deficiencies reported to management and the board.

# PCAOB

The PCAOB (created under SOX to oversee the activity of the auditors of public companies in the United States) expected the majority of US listed public companies to adopt the COSO framework as part of their SOX compliance activities. The PCAOB Auditing Standard No. 2, (now withdrawn and replaced by AS5) which dealt with the audit of internal control over financial reporting, assumed that the COSO framework (or one substantially like it) would have been adopted.

The PCAOB's Auditing Standard No. 2 contains, at paragraph 15, a statement that demonstrates close alignment with the Turnbull Guidance in the United Kingdom, and with the Basel 2 operational risk management requirements: 'Not all controls relevant to financial reporting are accounting controls. Accordingly, all controls that could materially affect financial reporting, including controls that focus primarily on the effectiveness and efficiency of operations or compliance with laws and regulations and also have a material effect on the reliability of financial reporting, are a part of internal control over financial reporting.'

Recognizing the fundamental role that IT systems play in financial reporting, COSO identifies two broad groups of IT systems control activities: general controls and application controls. General controls are those controls that ensure that the financial information from a company's application systems can be relied upon. General controls exist most commonly as part of an information security management system (such as that identified in ISO 27001[7]) or an IT controls system such as CobiT[8] (Control Objectives for Information and related Technology). Application controls are embedded in the software to detect or prevent unauthorized transactions. Such controls can be used to ensure the completeness, accuracy, validity and authorization of transactions.

The internal control environment must include 'information technology general controls over program development, program changes, computer operations, and access to programs and data which help ensure that specific controls over the processing of transactions are operating effectively'.[9]

While internal control is a process, its effectiveness (or otherwise) reflects the state or condition of the process at the time it is evaluated or is supposed to work. Auditing Standard No. 2, at paragraph 52, requires evaluation of the effectiveness of company-level controls at the outset of the audit engagement, on the basis that it is the company-level controls that have such a 'pervasive impact on controls at the process, transaction or application level'. These company-level controls include consistent policies and procedures and codes of conduct – all of which are at the heart of both ISO 27001 and CobiT. The PCAOB auditing standard specifically cross-references the existing *Consideration of Internal Control in a Financial Statement Audit*, issued by the AICPA in 1990, because it sets out clearly the effect of information technology on internal control over financial reporting.

# TURNBULL: GUIDANCE ON INTERNAL CONTROL

*The Turnbull Report – Internal Control: Guidance for directors on the Combined Code*, published by the Internal Control Working Party of the Institute of Chartered Accountants in England and Wales, was first published in September 1999. It was reviewed in 2005,[10] and *Internal Control: Revised guidance for directors on the Combined Code* was published by the Financial Reporting Council in October 2005 and applied for financial years beginning on or after 1 January 2006. It is not a formal document, in that companies are not required under the Listing Rules to demonstrate compliance with Turnbull. Turnbull is, however, the only UK-recognized guidance for companies on how to meet the requirements of clause C.2 of the Combined Code, and, for companies with a dual US listing, is a recognized internal control framework for the purposes of compliance with SOX section 404.

While there were no significant changes to the original version,[11] the revised guidance did recommend that boards continue reviewing their risk management activity and identified the need for the company's risk management framework to be interfaced with the requirements to produce an operating and financial review contained in the Companies Act 2004. The operating and financial review was renamed the business review in the Companies Act 2006.[12]

The Turnbull Guidance was designed to help boards of listed companies in:

▌ assessing how the company has applied Code principle C.2;

▌ implementing the requirements of Code provision C.2.1; and

▌ reporting on these matters to shareholders in the annual report and accounts.

The Turnbull Guidance says that a company's internal control system:

encompasses the policies, processes, tasks, behaviours and other aspects of a company that, taken together:

▌ Facilitate its effective and efficient operation by enabling it to respond appropriately to significant business, operational, financial, compliance and other risks to achieving the company's objectives. This includes the safeguarding of assets from inappropriate use and from loss or fraud, and ensuring that liabilities are identified and managed.

▌ Help ensure the quality of internal and external reporting. This requires the maintenance of proper records and processes that generate a flow of timely, relevant and reliable information from within and outside the organization.

▌ Help ensure compliance with applicable laws and regulations and also with internal policies with respect to the conduct of business.[13]

Turnbull's guidance on the composition of the internal control framework is actually very limited. In total, it says (clause 20):

A company's system of internal control will reflect its control environment which encompasses its organisational structure. The system will include:

■ control activities;

■ information and communications processes; and

■ processes for monitoring the continuing effectiveness of the system of internal control.

This means that organizations developing a system of internal control need to look elsewhere for guidance and, as suggested earlier in this chapter, the COSO internal control and integrated risk management frameworks are highly appropriate.

Turnbull, though, is particularly strong in its guidance on reviewing internal control activity. The responsibilities for doing this are set out in clause 24:

reviewing the effectiveness of internal control is an essential part of the board's responsibilities. The board will need to form its own view on effectiveness after due and careful enquiry based on the information and assurances provided to it. Management is accountable to the board for monitoring the system of internal control and for providing assurance to the board that it has done so.

Turnbull sets out the process for reviewing internal control in clauses 26 to 32. There should be ongoing review of the controls through the year as well as an annual board assessment of the entire internal control framework, preparatory to making its annual statement on internal control in the company's annual report and accounts. The Appendix to the Turnbull Guidance includes a list of questions that the 'board may wish to consider and discuss with management when regularly reviewing reports on internal control and carrying out its annual assessment. The questions are not intended to be exhaustive and will need to be tailored to the particular circumstances of the company.'

Clauses 33 to 38 provide guidance on the board's annual statement on internal control. These requirements are summarized in clause 34:

In its narrative statement of how the company has applied Code Principle C.2, the board should, as a minimum, disclose that there is an ongoing process for identifying, evaluating and managing the significant risks faced by the company, that it has been in place for the year under review and up to the date of approval of the annual report and accounts, that it is regularly reviewed by the board and accords with the guidance in this document.

# NOTES

1.  Turnbull Guidance, clause 1.
2.  Turnbull Guidance, clauses 16 to 18.
3.  www.pcaobus.org.
4.  See Chapter 2.
5.  The sponsoring organizations included the AICPA, the Institute of Internal Auditors, the Institute of Management Accountants and the American Accounting Association.
6.  *Internal Control – Integrated Framework*, Executive summary, www.coso.org.
7.  ISO/IEC 27001:2005 is the international Information Security Management System Standard, published by the International Standards Organization in Geneva.
8.  CobiT version 4.1, published by the IT Governance Institute in 2007.
9.  Paragraph 50 of PCAOB Auditing Standard No. 2.
10.  The Flint Review.
11.  Cross-references in the Turnbull Report 2003 to the Combined Code were not updated, so the Turnbull Guidance carries a footnote to the effect that Principle D.2, provision D.2.1 and provision D.2.2 of the old (1998) Code appear in the new (2003) Code as principle C.2, provision C.2.1 and (in an amended form) provision C.3.5. The Code references in the guidance on internal control should be read accordingly. These errors were corrected in the 2005 version of Turnbull, which also included a reordering of content and, therefore, of clause numbers.
12.  The business review is further discussed in Chapter 16.
13.  Turnbull Guidance, clause 19.

# 14

# The audit and auditors

Audit is an essential strand of corporate governance, and it is important to have a wide understanding of the audit framework. Financial auditors are independent accountants who are appropriately qualified and belong to their national professional institute[1] and are subject to codes of professional conduct and ethics.

## REGULATION OF AUDITORS

Part 2 of the Companies Act 1989 – which implemented the 8th EU Company Law Directive – contained provisions for the regulation of company auditors. Under these provisions, the Secretary of State (amongst other things) recognized accountancy bodies that met the statutory requirements for the supervision of auditors and also recognized professional audit qualifications that met the statutory requirements. In order to be eligible to act as a company auditor, a person must be appropriately qualified and registered with a recognized supervisory body.

After the Enron and WorldCom scandals, the UK government reviewed arrangements for the regulation of auditors and this led, in 2005, to the Financial Reporting Council (FRC)'s Professional Oversight Board for Accountancy (POBA) being made responsible for regulating auditors in the United Kingdom.[2]

POBA's three areas of responsibility are:

▪ setting accounting and audit standards;

▪ their enforcement or monitoring; and

▪ oversight of the major professional accountancy bodies.

As part of this change, the responsibility for setting auditor independence standards and monitoring the audit of listed companies and other significant entities was transferred from the professional accountancy bodies to the FRC.

The United Kingdom does not, however, develop audit standards on its own. International Standards on Auditing[3] (as distinct from accounting standards, which were discussed in Chapter 11), a code of ethics, and formal guidance on assurance engagements and other activities are produced and maintained under the auspices of the International Federation of Accountants (IFAC).[4]

# THE EU PERSPECTIVE

The European Commission has set up a European Group of Auditors' Oversight Bodies (EGAOB). The Group's role is to ensure effective coordination of public oversight systems of statutory auditors and audit firms within the European Union. It may provide technical input to the preparation of possible measures of the Commission implementing the directive on statutory audit, such as endorsement of the International Standards on Auditing or assessment of third countries' public oversight systems.

According to the EU directive on statutory audit, these public oversight systems will have the ultimate responsibility for the oversight of:

▌ the approval and registration of statutory auditors and audit firms;

▌ the adoption of standards on ethics, internal quality control of audit firms and auditing; and

▌ continuous education, quality assurance and investigative and disciplinary systems.

# STATUTORY AUDIT FRAMEWORK

In the United Kingdom, the statutory requirements relating to auditors are contained in Part 16 of the Companies Act 2006, which came into force with effect from 1 October 2007. They largely carry forward provisions of earlier Acts, although there were some significant changes.

Section 475, Requirement for audited accounts, simply says that a company's annual accounts for a financial year must be audited in accordance with the Act unless the company is:

▌ a small company (as defined in section 477)[5];

▌ a dormant company (as defined in section 480); or

▌ a non-profit-making company subject to public sector audit (under section 482).

Public companies are also required to appoint auditors (and the appointment can be made by either the directors or the shareholders in general meeting), and the auditors' appointment automatically ends at the end of the meeting at which the financial year's accounts are presented, unless they are reappointed. The Secretary of State has the power to appoint auditors, and fix their fees, if the company fails to do so.

Chapter 4 of Part 16 sets out the law regarding the removal, resignation and replacement of auditors, describing what must be done and how, and what rights the outgoing auditors will have. Any organization that is changing its auditors will have to go through these steps with care, and the advice of an experienced company secretary will be essential. In brief, the Act deliberately makes it difficult for a company to remove auditors whose actions it doesn't like, or from whose audit activities it fears exposure of some misdemeanour or other.

Section 493 of the Companies Act allows the Secretary of State to issue regulations requiring disclosure of the terms on which auditors are appointed and of related services provided by auditors. These provisions are aimed at the concern that auditors with a financially rewarding 'other services' relationship with a client may become inadequately objective in identifying and reporting weaknesses in internal control and other failings in their client.

Auditors are also entitled, under section 502, to receive copies of all notices or other information relating to shareholder general meetings, to attend general meetings, and to be heard – on any matter that concerns them as auditors – at any general meeting that they attend.

## THE AUDITOR'S LIABILITY

It should be noted that, under Chapter 6 of Part 16 of the Companies Act 2006, an auditor has unlimited liability in respect of any 'negligence, default, breach of duty or breach of trust in relation to the company of which he is the auditor occurring in the course of the audit of the accounts' (section 532), with the exception of two items:

▌ indemnity for costs of successfully defending proceedings (section 533); and

▌ liability limitation agreements (sections 534 to 536, which were a significant development in this Companies Act), which allow companies and their auditors to agree to limit their auditors' liability in respect of the accounts for not more than one specified year, so long as this limitation is approved by the members of the company and so long as the limitation is to a liability no less than is 'fair and reasonable' taking everything into account.

Any discussion about limiting the auditor's liability should take into account the requirement of the International Standard on Auditing (ISA 260) that requires auditors to 'communicate matters of governance interest arising from the audit of financial statements to those charged with governance of an entity'. The standard goes into more detail on this issue; the key point is that auditors are expected to raise issues with the governance body (usually the audit committee) of an entity, and executive management is not that governance entity.

## WHAT IS INTERNAL AUDIT?

The official definition of internal auditing of the Institute of Internal Auditors – United Kingdom and Ireland (IIA) is that 'internal auditing is an independent, objective assurance and consulting activity designed to add value and improve an organisation's operations. It helps an organisation accomplish its objectives by bringing a systematic, disciplined approach to evaluate and improve the effectiveness of risk management, control and governance processes.'[6] The internal audit function should deal with more than financial control. It should operate across all aspects of the internal control structure, dealing with all aspects of how effectively the organization's ERM framework is functioning, and this should include information technology, project management, health and safety, environment, corporate social responsibility, and so on.

Internal auditors look at how organisations are managing their risks. They provide the audit committee and the board of directors with information about whether risks have been identified, and how well they are being managed.

They are different to external auditors because they do not focus only on financial statements or financial risks: much of their work is looking at reputational, operational or strategic risks. They also give an independent opinion on whether internal controls – such as policies and procedures – put in place to manage these risks are actually working as intended.

They provide this information by, for example, checking that the assets of the organisation are being safeguarded; that operations are conducted effectively, efficiently and economically in accordance with the organisation's policies; that laws and regulations are complied with; and that records and reports are reliable and accurate. Internal auditors also review systems under development to ensure that good controls are built in, and may offer consultancy services or special reviews at the request of management.

The responsibility to manage risk always resides with management. Internal audit's role is to identify potential problem areas and recommend ways of improving risk management and internal control.

Internal audit may be provided by in-house staff, or an outsourced team. Either way, it is independent of the management structure, and reports directly to the audit committee. This independence gives it a unique and valuable perspective on risk management and internal control processes.

A professional, well resourced internal audit function is an integral and necessary part of an effective corporate governance framework: alongside the board, external audit, and executive management, internal audit is one of the four cornerstones of good governance.[7]

The IIA is the professional body in the United Kingdom and Ireland dedicated to the professional practice of internal auditing.

It is part of the global Institute of Internal Auditors, which sets the International Standards for the Professional Practice of Internal Auditing, and the Code of Ethics, which all members must agree to follow.

There can be a practical relationship between internal audit and the external, independent auditor. ISA 610, 'Considering the work of internal audit', says that the external auditor 'should consider the activities of internal auditing and their effect, if any, on external audit procedures'. The ISA goes on to say that the external auditor should recognize that internal audit is part of the overall internal control structure, and should sufficiently understand internal audit and its work to be able to identify and assess the risk of material misstatement of the financial statements. Depending on the external auditor's assessment of the competence of internal audit and the scope and quality of specific internal audit, the external auditor may use the work in internal audit in planning the external audit itself.

# WHAT IS IT AUDIT?

Companies have become more and more dependent on technology to support financial reporting and almost all aspects of business operations and to manage critical information assets. Continuous changes in technology and legislation create new exposures and requirements on organizations. This emphasizes the need for competency and experience in the proper evaluation of risks related to information technology and the adequacy of an organization's technology control structure. Information technology is fundamental to the work of auditors and to the audit process. It is therefore essential that auditors have a thorough understanding of the risks in IT systems that are relevant to the financial reports and to carry out, to the extent necessary, an IT audit.

An IT audit, though, is not necessarily the same as a financial statements audit. An evaluation of financial internal controls may or may not take place in an IT audit. Identification of and reliance on internal controls is a unique characteristic of a financial audit. An IT audit, on the other hand, is more likely to focus on the risks that are relevant to information assets and on assessing controls in order to reduce or mitigate these risks.

The International Systems Audit and Control Association (ISACA)[8] is the international body responsible for developing a specific IT controls audit framework,[9] which is now recognized worldwide. IT governance is an essential governance activity, and is covered separately in Chapter 18.

# NOTES

1. In England and Wales, the Institute of Chartered Accountants in England and Wales (ICAEW).
2. Companies Act 1989 (Delegation) Order 2005.
3. The International Auditing and Assurance Standards Board (IAASB) is the IFAC board responsible for setting and maintaining international standards on auditing, review, assurance, quality control and related services for the accountancy profession's auditing activity.
4. www.ifac.org.
5. It can't be a public company (and there are other limitations), it must have turnover in that year of not more than £5.6 million, *and* the balance sheet total must be not more than £2.8 million.

6. The IIA, Code of Ethics and International Standards.
7. What is internal audit? This answer is the one provided by the IIA, on its website at www.iia.org.uk.
8. www.isaca.org.
9. CobiT, IAOW in version 4.1.

# 15

# The audit committee

The UK requirement for an audit committee is part of the non-statutory corporate governance framework. The Combined Code deals with the subject in Section C.3, 'Audit committee and auditors'. It should also be noted that the Listing Rules require the company's auditors to review and report on the company's application of Combined Code principles C.3.1 to C.3.7.

The main principle set out in the Code is that the board should establish formal and transparent arrangements for considering how they should apply the financial reporting and internal control principles and for maintaining an appropriate relationship with the company's auditors.

It also, of course, provides substantial additional guidance on the role and workings of audit committees in the Smith Report, which is discussed later in this chapter.

## AUDIT COMMITTEE

The Companies Act 2006 (unlike the Sarbanes–Oxley Act) does not require companies to set up audit committees. This is a Combined Code principle, C.3. The main principle is that the board should establish an audit committee of at least three or in the case of smaller companies two members, who should all be independent, non-executive directors. The board should satisfy itself that at least one member of the audit committee has recent and relevant financial experience; this is usually achieved by ensuring that one of the board members is a current or recent CFO of a similar organization who is ready and willing to take on the responsibility. There have been instances where, because none of the directors had adequate financial experience, an approach has been developed that involves the appointment of an alternate director who does have the necessary experience and for whom attendance mechanisms have been designed to enable audit committee meetings to be chaired and for the audit committee to communicate with the board and the members.

Provision C.3.2 says that the main role and responsibilities of the audit committee should be set out in written terms of reference. There is a set of model terms of reference for an audit committee in Appendix 5. The Combined Code is clear that the terms of reference for the audit committee should include:

▮ monitoring the integrity of the financial statements of the company, and any formal announcements relating to the company's financial performance, and reviewing significant financial reporting judgements contained in them;

▮ reviewing the company's internal financial controls and, unless expressly addressed by a separate board risk committee composed of independent directors, or by the board itself, reviewing the company's internal control and risk management systems;

▮ monitoring and reviewing the effectiveness of the company's internal audit function;

▮ making recommendations to the board, for it to put to the shareholders for their approval in general meeting, in relation to the appointment, reappointment and removal of the external auditor and to approve the remuneration and terms of engagement of the external auditor;

▮ reviewing and monitoring the external auditor's independence and objectivity and the effectiveness of the audit process, taking into consideration relevant UK professional and regulatory requirements;

▮ developing and implementing policy on the engagement of the external auditor to supply non-audit services, taking into account relevant ethical guidance regarding the provision of non-audit services by the external audit firm; and

▮ reporting to the board, identifying any matters in respect of which it considers that action or improvement is needed and making recommendations as to the steps to be taken.

Under provision C.3.3, the terms of reference of the audit committee, including its role and the authority delegated to it by the board, should be made available on request and be published on the company's website. A separate section of the annual report should describe the work of the committee in discharging its responsibilities.

C.3.4 provides for overview of the whistle-blowing arrangements: the audit committee should review arrangements by which staff of the company may, in confidence, raise concerns about possible improprieties in matters of financial reporting or other matters. The audit committee's objective should be to ensure that arrangements are in place for the proportionate and independent investigation of such matters and for appropriate follow-up action.

## Whistle-blowing

There is an obvious linkage between provision C.3.4 of the Combined Code and the UK Public Interest Disclosure Act 1998,[1] which came into force on 2 July 1999 and was designed to encourage people to raise concerns about malpractice in the workplace and to help organizations respond. The Act protects employees, trainees, agency staff, contractors, homeworkers and trainees from dismissal and victimization in the workplace when they raise genuine concerns about crime, civil offences (including negligence, breach of contract and breach of administrative law), miscarriage of justice, danger to health and safety or to the environment and the cover-up of any of these.

# APPOINTING AUDITORS

C.3.6 provides for the audit committee to have primary responsibility for making a recommendation to the board on the appointment, reappointment and removal of the external auditors. If the board does not accept the audit committee's recommendation, it should include in the annual report, and in any papers recommending appointment or reappointment, a statement from the audit committee explaining the recommendation and should set out reasons why the board has taken a different position.

C.3.7 echoes section 493 of the Companies Act 2006, and recommends that the annual report explain to shareholders how, if the auditor provides non-audit services, auditor objectivity and independence are safeguarded.

# INTERNAL AUDITORS

C.3.5 of the Combined Code provides for the audit committee to monitor and review the effectiveness of the internal audit activities. Where there is no internal audit function, the audit committee should consider annually whether there is a need for an internal audit function and make a recommendation to the board, and the reasons for the absence of such a function should be explained in the relevant section of the annual report. The appropriate basis for making a decision for or against an internal audit function should be the result of a risk assessment that takes into account both the risks that can be controlled through such a function and the costs of staffing and running it effectively.

Key recommendations in the IIA's position statement *Audit Committees and Internal Auditors* include:

▌ The head of internal audit should have access to the chair of the audit committee.

▌ The head of internal audit and the chair of the audit committee should have the opportunity to meet alone outside of the normal meetings.

▌ The head of internal audit should report to the chair of the audit committee all significant concerns that he or she may have over the adequacy and effectiveness of internal controls and risk management activities within the organization.

▌ There should be provision for internal auditors to have access to the audit committee in private at least once a year to raise any unresolved issues of concern.

## NOTE

1.  See http://www.pcaw.co.uk/legislation/legislation.html.

# 16

# Relations with shareholders

Corporate governance is, essentially, about the relationship between a company and its shareholders. The statutory framework within which companies have to manage their relations with their shareholders is contained in the Companies Act 2006, which is primarily about the obligations and statutory requirements on the company. The non-statutory framework, which is contained in the Combined Code on Corporate Governance, sets out obligations on the company as well as on its institutional shareholders.

## STATUTORY FRAMEWORK FOR RELATIONS WITH SHAREHOLDERS

The Companies Act 2006 has extensive provisions dealing with the rights of members of the company. Members' rights are primarily expressed in two ways: through resolutions passed by meetings of members, and in receiving specific information and reports from the directors, which they are then entitled to approve or reject. Where a company has different classes of shares, there may well be different rights attached to each class, and separate shareholders' meetings may need to be convened in relation to each class of shares.

The company secretary has a key role to play in ensuring that the directors are aware of the various statutory aspects of their relations with shareholders, and should be in a position to advise the board on precisely what steps are required in relation to each type of activity.

## Resolutions and meetings

The Companies Act, Part 13, deals with resolutions and meetings. Resolutions are the mechanism for authorizing and implementing changes to the company's articles, the reappointment of directors, the appointment of auditors, political donations[1] and the approval of various reports.

There are two types of resolution, an ordinary resolution and a special resolution. Resolutions of private companies may be written resolutions[2] or resolutions put to a vote at a meeting of shareholders; resolutions of public companies cannot be written resolutions. Votes in meetings may be on a show of hands of those entitled to vote or those who have a valid proxy vote.

An ordinary resolution is one that can be passed by a simple majority of votes (section 282); a special resolution is one that requires a majority of 75 per cent (section 283). A special resolution must be so designated in the notice that called the meeting.

The Act authorizes directors to call general meetings of shareholders (section 302); it also enables any group representing at least 10 per cent of the shares to require the directors to call a general meeting (section 303), and this ensures that the members are able to take action as and when appropriate to deal with specific issues of concern. If the directors do not call a meeting when required to do so, the members may then call it themselves (section 305) and at the company's expense, and if all else fails, a court may order a meeting (section 306).

General meetings of both private and public companies may be called on 14 days' notice (section 307), although a public company's annual general meeting requires 21 days' notice. A company's articles may require longer notice periods, in which case those will prevail. Shorter notice may be given, if at least 95 per cent[3] of a public company's members agree to the short notice. Notice of a general meeting may be given in writing, by e-mail or by publication on a website (sections 308 and 309). The notice period for a special resolution, though, is 28 days (section 312).

The Companies Act also sets out how meetings should proceed. The quorum for meetings, the chairmanship of the meeting, and how votes are to be taken and decisions recorded are usually all contained in a company's articles. Where they are not, then the provisions of sections 318 *et seq* will apply.

## Accounts and reports

Part 15 of the Companies Act 2006 contains the various requirements for companies to report to their members. For reporting purposes, the Act differentiates[4] between small companies, private companies that are not small companies, and public companies, quoted and unquoted.

Companies are required to keep accounting records[5] in relation to the company's financial year; and there are rules covering changes to the accounting reference date by which the financial year is determined.[6] To ensure that directors don't hide critical information about company expenditure, there is a range of information that must be included in the notes to the annual accounts, including information about related undertakings[7] and data about employee numbers and costs and directors' remuneration.[8]

The annual accounts must include a directors' report,[9] which must state the amount of the proposed dividend and must contain (other than for small companies) a business review.

## Business review

The requirement for a company to include a business review[10] first surfaced in the Companies Act 2004, and it was originally described as an operating and financial review (OFR). While the requirements of the OFR have been scaled down, the business review is still a detailed document that is designed to help a company's members assess how the directors have performed their duty under section 172 of the Act (duty to promote the success of the company). Specifically:

(3)   The business review must contain –
    (a)   a fair review of the company's business, and
    (b)   a description of the principal risks and uncertainties facing the company.

(4)   The review required is a balanced and comprehensive analysis of –
    (a)   the development and performance of the company's business during the financial year, and
    (b)   the position of the company's business at the end of that year, consistent with the size and complexity of the business.

(5)   In the case of a quoted company the business review must, to the extent necessary for an understanding of the development, performance or position of the company's business, include –

(a)  the main trends and factors likely to affect the future development, performance and position of the company's business; and

(b)  information about –

   (i)  environmental matters (including the impact of the company's business on the environment),

   (ii)  the company's employees, and

   (iii)  social and community issues including information about any policies of the company in relation to those matters and the effectiveness of those policies; and

(c)  subject to subsection (11), information about persons with whom the company has contractual or other arrangements which are essential to the business of the company.

If the review does not contain information of each kind mentioned in paragraphs (b)(i), (ii) and (iii) and (c), it must state which of those kinds of information it does not contain.

(6)  The review must, to the extent necessary for an understanding of the development, performance or position of the company's business, include –

(a)  analysis using financial key performance indicators, and

(b)  where appropriate, analysis using other key performance indicators, including information relating to environmental matters and employee matters.

'Key performance indicators' means factors by reference to which the development, performance or position of the company's business can be measured effectively.

There are also specific requirements contained in the rest of Part 15 of the Act dealing with issues such as the periods set out by law for the filing of accounts, for delivering copies of accounts to members, for the format of those accounts, including their being signed by a director on behalf of the board, for abbreviated accounts and for non-statutory accounts.

## Shareholder actions

Shareholders have the right, at a number of points in the Companies Act, to bring an action against their company. These include circumstances where directors have caused the company to make political donations that have not been authorized by the members (sections 370 to 373).[11]

Part 2 of the Companies Act allows for what are called 'derivative claims'. A derivative claim:

> may be brought only in respect of a cause of action arising from an actual or proposed act or omission involving negligence, default, breach of duty or breach of trust by a director of the company.
>
>   The cause of action may be against the director or another person (or both).

Members also have the right to require the company to publish on its website concerns that they might have in relation to the audit of the company's accounts[12] and, as described above, to propose resolutions of their own.

# SHAREHOLDER RELATIONS – NON-STATUTORY FRAMEWORK

While there are many circumstances in which it is entirely adequate for a private company to do no more than the statutory minimum in terms of shareholder relations, quoted public companies are expected to do far more.

The Listing Rules contain specific provisions (Listing Principles 3, 4 and 5) in relation to how a company deals with its shareholders and with the market generally. In addition, listed companies have to comply with the new transparency rules.

## Disclosure Rules and Transparency Rules (DTR)

New transparency rules were introduced by the FSA on 20 January 2007 to implement the EU Transparency Directive in the United Kingdom.

The United Kingdom Listing Authority disclosure rules are called the 'Disclosure Rules and Transparency Rules'. They require companies with securities admitted to trading on a regulated market to produce annual and half-yearly financial reports (including financial statements, a management report and a responsibility statement), and for equity issuers only, two other (ie quarterly) interim management statements a year. The periodic financial reporting requirements apply for financial periods beginning on or after 20 January 2007.

The DTR is dealt with under the following headings:[13]

| Reference code | Title |
| --- | --- |
| DTR 1 | Introduction |
| DTR 1A | Introduction (Transparency rules) |
| DTR 2 | Disclosure and control of inside information by issuers |
| DTR 3 | Transactions by persons discharging managerial responsibilities and their connected persons |
| DTR 4 | Periodic Financial Reporting |
| DTR 5 | Vote holder and issuer notification rules |
| DTR6 | Continuing obligations and access to information |
| DTR Transchedule | Transitional Provisions |

Transparency is essential to corporate governance. Good practice in shareholder relations, as contained in the Combined Code on Corporate Governance, Section D, involves a proactive approach to communicating with shareholders, not just by the CEO and finance director, but by the chairman, the non-executive directors and the senior independent non-executive.

The Code identifies two main principles:

1.   There should be a dialogue with shareholders based on the mutual understanding of objectives. The board as a whole has responsibility for ensuring that a satisfactory dialogue with shareholders takes place. [D.1]

2.   The board should use the AGM to communicate with investors and to encourage their participation. [D.2]

Other than at the AGM, it is impractical for companies to have the sort of dialogue envisaged by the Code with all its individual shareholders. The key shareholders with whom the company should have dialogue are their institutional shareholders and investors. An institutional investor can be defined as an investor, such as a bank, insurance company, retirement fund, hedge fund or mutual fund, that is financially sophisticated and makes large investments, often held in very large portfolios of investments.

While the Code recognizes that most of the contact between institutional investors and the company will be with the CEO and finance director, the chairman is also tasked with ensuring that 'the views of shareholders are communicated to the board as a whole. The chairman should discuss governance and strategy with major shareholders.' Non-executive directors should have the opportunity to attend meetings with major shareholders (who are entitled to request their attendance). More controversially, and something that needs to be handled with tact and sensitivity by all the individuals involved, the senior independent director is expected to attend sufficient meetings with enough 'major shareholders to listen to their views in order to help develop a balanced understanding of the issues and concerns of major shareholders' (D.1.1).

Provision D.1.2 recommends that the board describe in the annual report all the steps it has taken to ensure that the members of the board, and in particular the non-executive directors, have developed an understanding of the views of major shareholders.

In terms of the AGM, the Code does not advance much further than the statutory requirements. Provision D.2.2, which recommends that there should be a separate motion on each substantive issue, and a separate motion to approve the report and accounts, is only advising against attempting to concatenate a number of issues into a single resolution, which would be manifestly bad practice. D.2.2.1 deals with the proper tallying, recording and reporting of abstentions and proxy votes cast.

Provision D.2.3 recommends that the chairman arrange for all the non-executives and the chairmen of the audit, remuneration and nomination committees to be available at the AGM to answer questions.

Provision D.2.4 recommends a notice period for the AGM that is longer than the statutory 21-day minimum notice period and recommends that the notice of the AGM and related papers be sent to shareholders at least 20 working days (ie approximately 28 calendar days) before the planned date of the meeting.

The Smith Guidance (which is not part of the Code itself) echoes the recommendation that the chairman of the audit committee should be present at the AGM, and also says (at clause 5.1) that the 'terms of reference of the audit committee, including its role and the authority delegated to it by the board, should be made available. A separate section in the annual report should describe the work of the committee in discharging those responsibilities.'

Finally, the Listing Rules require quoted companies to provide a statement, in their annual reports, that describes how they have complied with the Code. Schedule C (Disclosure of corporate governance arrangements) lists, for convenience, all the provisions for which the Code has specific disclosure requirements.

## Institutional shareholders

The Combined Code also requires institutional shareholders to interact proactively and objectively with the companies in which they are invested. There are three main principles for institutional shareholders to observe:

1.  Institutional shareholders should enter into a dialogue with companies based on the mutual understanding of objectives. [E.1]

2.  When evaluating companies' governance arrangements, particularly those relating to board structure and composition, institutional shareholders should give due weight to all relevant factors drawn to their attention. [E.2]

3.  Institutional shareholders have a responsibility to make considered use of their votes. [E.3]

The Combined Code explicitly recommends that institutional investors should not accept a 'box-ticking' approach to corporate governance, and that their consideration of disclosures made by the company in relation to the Code should take into account the 'size and complexity of the company and the nature of the risks and challenges it faces' (supporting principle to E.2).

The Combined Code recommends (supporting principle to E.1) that City institutions should follow 'The responsibilities of institutional shareholders and agents – statement of principles', which was drawn up by the Institutional Shareholders' Committee (ISC), whose associations represent virtually all UK institutional investors.[14]

The principles were the first comprehensive statement of best practice governing the responsibilities of institutional shareholders and investment managers in relation to the companies in which they invest:

> They aim to secure value for ultimate beneficiaries – pension scheme members and individual savers – through consistent monitoring of the performance of those companies. This is to be backed up by direct engagement where appropriate. The principles make it clear that if companies persistently fail to respond to concerns, institutional shareholders and investment managers, ISC members will vote against the Board at general meetings.

> The principles set out best practice for institutional shareholders and investment managers, under which they will:

- Maintain and publish statements of their policies in respect of active engagement with the companies in which they invest;

- Monitor the performance of and maintain an appropriate dialogue with those companies;

- Intervene where necessary;

- Evaluate the impact of their policies; and

- In the case of investment managers, report back to the clients on whose behalf they invest.[15]

# NOTES

1. See Part 14, Companies Act 2006.
2. The statutory requirements around written resolutions are contained in sections 288 to 300 of the Companies Act 2006; readers who wish more information on this subject are recommended to start with the identified sections of the Act.
3. 90 per cent for a private company.
4. The definitions of each type of company for the purposes of this Part of the Act are contained in sections 381 to 385.
5. See sections 386 to 389, and Chapter 11 of this book.
6. See sections 390 to 392.
7. See sections 409 to 410.
8. See sections 411 to 413.
9. See Chapter 5 of Part 15 of the Act.
10. See section 417, from which the excerpt describing the required contents of the business review has been taken. This section also contains provisions that allow the directors not to include information if, in their opinion, it would be seriously prejudicial to the interests of the company or an individual. These 'opt-outs' are designed so that companies do not have to reveal competitive information, not so that the directors can hide information from the shareholders.
11. A donation to a trade union is not a political donation (section 374).
12. See sections 527 to 531.
13. http://fsahandbook.info/FSA/html/handbook/LR/9/Annex1
14. The ISC is a forum that allows the UK's institutional shareholding community to exchange views and, on occasion, coordinate their

activities in support of the interests of UK investors. Its constituent members are the Association of British Insurers (ABI), the Association of Investment Companies (AIC), the Investment Management Association (IMA) and the National Association of Pension Funds (NAPF).

15.   ISC press release accompanying the launch of the principles.

# 17

# Corporate governance in the UK public sector

Corporate governance in the public sector is still very immature, and the final model for applying a now relatively mature and well-tested private sector model of corporate governance to the public sector is still evolving.

Corporate governance is understood differently across the public sector than it is in the private one. Public sector organizations do not have shareholders, although they certainly do have stakeholders. There is usually a public interest that is served by the existence of such an organization, rather than the simpler and clearer requirement of a private sector organization for profit maximization. Furthermore, public sector organizations operate in complex legislative, political and local contexts, in which they have to make and implement sometimes difficult and sometimes unpopular decisions.

## THE UK PUBLIC SECTOR

The UK public sector can be thought of as comprising central government, local government, executive agencies, non-departmental public bodies (NDPBs)[1] and public–private sector partnerships, each of which has its own particular set of governance characteristics.

The theoretical approaches to corporate governance that were discussed in Chapter 1 need to be extended, when considering the public sector, to include what might be called the 'stakeholder approach' to corporate governance. In principle, this theory is that boards of NDPBs or even central government departments might recruit board members (non-executive directors – NEDs) to represent major stakeholders in the activity of the organization, so that their views are seen to be taken into account.

The recruitment of stakeholders on to boards creates evident conflicts of interest for those NEDs when relationships with their own organization have to be addressed, and the chairman's role is the sometimes tricky one of ensuring that directors meet their primary responsibility – which is to the company – while at the same time enabling stakeholder views to be taken into account.

# THE NOLAN REPORT – THE COMMITTEE ON STANDARDS IN PUBLIC LIFE

In 1994, the then prime minister, John Major, invited a committee chaired by Lord Nolan, to inquire into 'standards in British public life'. The Nolan Committee concentrated on Members of Parliament, ministers and civil servants, executive quangos and NHS bodies.

The Nolan Committee's report commenced with a set of general principles (*The Seven Principles of Public Life*), and while much of the report is specific to Members of Parliament, ministers and civil servants, much of it is also relevant to organizational and corporate governance in the public sector.

The Committee's work was reaffirmed in January 2000 as part of the Cabinet Office's Quinquennial Review of the Committee, which concluded that there was a 'continuing need to monitor the ethical environment and to respond to issues of concern, which may arise'. The Nolan Committee has become the Committee on Standards in Public Life,[2] and it produced its eleventh report (which dealt with Electoral Commission reform) on 18 January 2007.

## The Seven Principles of Public Life[3]

### Selflessness
Holders of public office should take decisions solely in terms of the public interest. They should not do so in order to gain financial or other material benefits for themselves, their family, or their friends.

### Integrity
Holders of public office should not place themselves under any financial or other obligation to outside individuals or organisations that might influence them in the performance of their official duties.

### Objectivity
In carrying out public business, including making public appointments, awarding contracts, or recommending individuals for rewards and benefits, holders of public office should make choices on merit.

### Accountability
Holders of public office are accountable for their decisions and actions to the public and must submit themselves to whatever scrutiny is appropriate to their office.

### Openness
Holders of public office should be as open as possible about all the decisions and actions that they take. They should give reasons for their decisions and restrict information only when the wider public interest clearly demands.

### Honesty
Holders of public office have a duty to declare any private interests relating to their public duties and to take steps to resolve any conflicts arising in a way that protects the public interest.

### Leadership
Holders of public office should promote and support these principles by leadership and example.

These principles apply to all aspects of public life. The Committee set them out, it said, for the benefit of all who serve the public in any way.

One recommendation of the Nolan Committee was the creation of a public appointments commissioner to make sure that appropriate standards were met in the appointment of members of NDPBs. The government accepted the recommendation, and the Office of the Commissioner for Public Appointments was established in November 1995. Board members of NDPBs are now usually appointed following the Code of Practice of the Commissioner for Public Appointments (OCPA).[4]

While the Nolan Committee had a major influence on the formalization of the UK approach to public sector governance, the development of a common understanding across the public sector of corporate governance is more practically traced back to the Cadbury Report, whose evolution was discussed in Chapter 5, which identified the principles of good governance as integrity, openness and accountability. The subsequent reports on corporate governance in the private sector – the Higgs Report on non-executive directors and the Smith Report on audit committees – have also had an impact on the public sector's understanding of the topic.

Many public sector organizations face common governance challenges relating to the role and importance of non-executives, the effective use of information, engaging users and the public, and the balance between local and national priorities.

# UK AUDIT COMMISSION ON UK PUBLIC SECTOR CORPORATE GOVERNANCE

The UK Audit Commission, a publicly funded but statutorily independent body that has a history of making independent, objective reports on the broad range of issues that fall within its remit, produced a report in 2003 on public sector corporate governance. In this report, it defined corporate governance (in the public sector) as: 'The framework of accountability to users, stakeholders and the wider community, within which organisations take decisions, and lead and control their functions, to achieve their objectives.'

This report went on to describe good corporate governance as a combination of:

the 'hard' factors – robust systems and processes – with the 'softer' characteristics of effective leadership and high standards of behaviour. It incorporates both strong internal characteristics and the ability to scan and work effectively in the external environment. The internal combination of 'hard' and 'soft' characteristics involves:

- **leadership** that establishes a vision for organisations, generates clarity about strategy and objectives, roles and responsibilities, and fosters professional relationships;

- **culture** based on openness and honesty, in which decisions and behaviours can be challenged and accountability is clear;

▌ supporting accountability through **systems and processes**, such as risk management, financial management, performance management and internal controls. They must be robust and produce reliable information to enable better decisions to be reached about what needs to be done in order to achieve objectives; and

▌ **external focus** on the needs of service users and the public, reflecting diverse views in decision making, producing greater ownership among stakeholders and maintaining clarity of purpose.

The Audit Commission's report then went on to describe decision making in the public sector, which it recognized:

> always involves risk, but this risk is reduced when an open culture exists in which challenge is accepted and supported. This challenge and openness must be underpinned by robust performance, financial and information management systems, the effective use of risk management and an accountability framework that is based on a clear communication and understanding across the organisation of roles and responsibilities.

Equally, the Audit Commission stressed that:

> the importance of effective leadership in ensuring good governance is clear from inspection reports and from other reports generated across the public sector. Ultimately, leaders are responsible for achieving the right balance of hard and soft factors and are accountable for the decisions they take, or fail to take. They set the strategy for organisations and give it a sense of direction and purpose. The relationships between those carrying out executive and non-executive roles are fundamental to setting the tone for the cultural aspects of organisations that can never be codified or set out in detailed guidance, but which are immediately recognisable to those who work in or deal with them.

In both the private and public sectors, the drive to outsource services is increasingly important. In the public sector, particularly, more and more services are delivered through contracts between public, private and voluntary sector organizations, and through more informal collaborations with a range of partners across all sectors.

Organizations are not that easily able to ensure that partnerships and contracts are effective unless their corporate governance arrangements are also effective. Managers who have a vested interest in representing that their outsourcing decisions were good ones, and that they are delivering real value for the public sector purse, are not the people who should be responsible for reviewing and assessing contract value. A key aspect of good public sector corporate governance is how it oversees the selection of external providers and manages the delivery of publicly funded contracts.

# WHO IS RESPONSIBLE FOR CORPORATE GOVERNANCE IN THE PUBLIC SECTOR?

Across the public sector as a whole (particularly in local government, reflecting the democratic foundations of local authorities), titles are not always consistently applied. The key governance roles are usually described in terms of the responsibilities of executive directors and non-executive directors, applying terminology widely used in the private sector.

In this book, as in the 2003 Audit Commission report, the terms 'executive' and 'executive director' are applied to the corporate management team (the chief executive and senior service directors) in local authorities and other public sector entities. The term 'non-executive' or 'non-executive director' is applied to those roles carried out by elected councillors; it has to be borne in mind, however, that elected councillors do also have a role in decision making on a number of committees and it may in practice be difficult to argue that they have the same level of 'independence' as is expected of a private sector NED. In the police service, 'executives' are the chief constable and his or her senior management team; and the 'non-executive' function is filled by members of the police authority. In many executive agencies and NDPBs, all board members except the chief executive officer are non-executives; the chief executive officer and his or her senior management team are the executives.

# LOCAL GOVERNMENT

The governance of local authorities is driven by the Local Government Act 2000. All UK councils now have constitutions that set out their standing orders and codes of conduct; they appoint monitoring officers and establish standards committees.

Local authority decision makers are directly accountable to their local electorate. As a result, decision making in local government is generally far more transparent than in the private sector or in other parts of the public sector. A combative party political environment can, however, include highlighting of poor performance or mistakes in order to denigrate an opposing political party in the public's mind; this is not the same as good governance.

# HEALTH

The Department of Health (DoH) has pushed effective corporate governance for NHS trusts for many years. It has issued intricately pre-scribed codes of governance and conduct and has rolled out a programme of controls assurance. The term 'corporate governance', however, has a narrower focus in the NHS than in other sectors. The key areas of focus are providing high-quality information for decision making, enhancing the role of non-executives and communicating effectively with service users and with the public. 'The clinician's traditional values are professional autonomy, the focus on individual patients, the desire for self-regulation, and the role of evidence-based practice. In contrast, managers' values are the emphasis on populations, the need for public accountability, the preoccupation with systems and the allocation of resources.'[5]

NHS trusts are governed by unitary boards with an equal number (five) of executive and non-executive directors, plus a chair. These unitary boards bring together clinicians and managers, as well as NEDs. But the committee structures beneath board level usually reflect a clear separation of 'corporate governance' and 'clinical governance'. The existence of these governance 'streams' is a distinguishing feature of the NHS and a legacy of the historical autonomy that consultants have had when taking clinical decisions.

Clinical care is the core business of the NHS and clinical governance has achieved much in terms of promoting better care for patients. But chairs and chief executives who contributed to our research are concerned about some consultants' unwillingness to be held to account by managers and non-executives for professional decisions. One chief executive from a primary care trust said 'You tread on clinicians' toes at your peril'. The consequences of this are that the clinical arm of the organisation wants to, and often does, deliver excellent clinical care to some individual patients, but not always with due regard for equity, finance and the bigger community picture.[6]

The Audit Commission expressed concern about the quality of information used in the NHS for decision making:

> the poor quality of information, both about finances and about clinical practice and patient care, remains one of the key governance risks that the NHS faces. The Audit Commission's recent reports on the quality of data in the NHS show that, while it has improved, data quality still has some way to go before it can be said to provide a robust basis on which decisions can be taken. In the NHS, it is not always clear that the board asks the right questions and this, in part, is because the NHS collects a vast array of data that is not always presented in a context that is meaningful to the organisation as a whole. The new Commission for Health Audit and Inspection will review the effectiveness with which providers use information in clinical and managerial decision making.
>
> Inadequate information in the NHS reduces the clarity that supports the decision making that is necessary for effective accountability. This creates the conditions in which severe malpractice can occur, including the deliberate falsification of waiting list information. The Audit Commission's work suggests that this occurs rarely, but at the same time, most auditors report a lack of confidence in the reliability and accuracy of reported information. The effect of both on public trust and confidence should not be underestimated.

# TARGETS, REGULATION, INSPECTION AND AUDIT

## Targets

Reactions to national targets vary, often according to how long organizations have existed and the relationship they have with their communities. Organizations with greater accountability to the local community, such as local government and the police, are more resistant to national targets on the grounds that they constrain their independence and conflict with local priorities.

On the other hand, those organizations that are locally managed within a national service, such as primary care trusts (PCTs), healthcare trusts and the newly restructured probation service, are more likely to respond to national frameworks and targets. Research conducted for the Audit Commission showed that:

> while board members and executives would like national policy frameworks to be simplified and clarified, many believe that national priorities *per se* are not inherently in conflict with local priorities, such as mental health, cancer or reducing re-offending. However, they do point to the need for greater freedom in how they deliver improvement against the targets. The way that trusts need to deal with cancer, for example, can differ in different areas. Targets should focus effort on outcomes; the way in which the outcomes are achieved should be more a matter for local discretion.

## Inspection and audit

Regulation from either central government or independent regulators provides the framework, through statute or guidance, within which public sector organizations operate. It helps to ensure that minimum acceptable standards of service are met. Inspection is an important part of the accountability framework, providing information on levels of performance and improvement progress to both policy makers and the public. External audit is an essential element in the process of accountability for public money. It can also make an important contribution to the stewardship of public resources and make recommendations about how some aspects of corporate governance could be improved.

# THE GOOD GOVERNANCE STANDARD FOR PUBLIC SERVICES

CIPFA (the Chartered Institute of Public Finance and Accountancy) is one of the leading professional accountancy bodies in the United Kingdom and the only one that specializes in the public sector. It is responsible for the education and training of professional accountants and for their regulation through the setting and monitoring of professional standards. Uniquely among the professional accountancy bodies in the United Kingdom, CIPFA has responsibility for setting accounting standards for a significant part of the economy, namely local government.

CIPFA's members work in public service bodies, the national audit agencies and major accountancy firms. CIPFA also provides a range of high-quality advisory, information, training and consultancy services to public service organizations. CIPFA claims to be the leading independent commentator on managing and accounting for public money.

Early in 2004, the Office of Public Management (OPM) and CIPFA, in partnership with the Joseph Rowntree Foundation, established an independent commission to develop a common code for good governance across the public services. The resulting Independent Commission on Good Governance for Public Services is chaired by Sir Alan Langlands, vice-chancellor at the University of Dundee and former chief executive of the National Health Service.

The Commission was responsible for producing *The Good Governance Standard for Public Services*.[7] This standard provides a guidance for everyone in the public sector in understanding and applying common governance principles, and also assessing the strengths and weaknesses of their current governance practice and seeking to improve it.

# AUDIT COMMITTEES IN THE PUBLIC SECTOR

HM Treasury published, in October 2003, the *Audit Committees Handbook and Policy Principles*. This required all central government departments, executive agencies and NDPBs to have an audit committee, whose role is to support the accounting office (and only secondarily the board of the NDPB) in monitoring corporate governance and systems of internal control. It is the organization's accounting officer who is responsible for establishing the audit committee, not the board. The audit committee should, for preference, be chaired by a non-executive. Unlike the far more stringent private sector principles, the public sector principles allow executive directors to serve on the audit committee. In a number of other respects, the public sector principles diverge from the Combined Code.

# PUBLIC SECTOR RISK MANAGEMENT

HM Treasury's 'Orange Book', *Management of Risk: Principles and concepts*, has been published. This replaces the previous edition of the 'Orange Book', *Management of Risk: A strategic overview*, issued under cover of a formal letter to a principal finance officer (PFO) dated 30 April 2001.

This publication continues to provide broad-based general guidance on the principles of risk management, but has been enhanced to reflect lessons learned about public sector risk management through the experience of the last few years. It should be read and used in conjunction with other relevant advice such as the 'Green Book', which contains specific advice on 'Appraisal and evaluation in central government', the Office of Government Commerce's 'Management of risk', which provides more detailed guidance on the practical application of the principles and concepts contained in this publication, and guidance provided by the Treasury's Risk Support Team as part of the Risk Programme.

Chapter 21 of HM Treasury's *Government Accounting* (published May 2003) is titled 'Risk management and the statement on internal control'. It applies to departments, executive agencies and NDPBs, amongst others. It sets out the basis on which the organization's accounting officer is responsible for signing the statement on internal control (SIC).

# PUBLIC–PRIVATE SECTOR PARTNERSHIPS

Partnerships between the public sector (eg a Regional Development Agency) and the private sector (companies that have a specific interest in an issue that is being promoted by the public sector organization) are usually constituted in the form of companies limited by guarantee. The stakeholder theory of corporate governance is likely to apply, and the board is likely to consist of representatives of the partner organizations.

These organizations are usually in receipt of substantial sums of public money, and there is therefore an expectation that their standards of corporate governance will at least match those of the private sector. For most such bodies, the applicable private sector guidance will be the *QCA Corporate Governance Guidance for AIM Companies*,[8] rather than the Combined Code on Corporate Governance. This reflects the reality that most public–private partnerships are relatively small organizations and that their board structure is such that it is virtually impossible for their non-executive directors to meet the independence criteria of the Combined Code, or for the board to comply with the guidance about the balance of non-executive and executive directors. The QCA Guidance is succinct, clear and comprehensive, and this should be the corporate governance starting point for most public–private partnerships.

It is also often the case that the non-executive directors, appointed to represent their own organizations on the partnership board, will have little appropriate business or governance experience; their exposure, under the

Companies Act 2006, is not however any different from that of the more experienced directors that the company is (hopefully) employing in an executive capacity.

This means, in my opinion, that the executive directors and, particularly, the company auditors have an enhanced duty of care in respect of the company; an effective audit committee, working with an external auditor appropriately experienced in the sector, is essential to the short- and long-term governance effectiveness of the board of any public–private partnership.

# NOTES

1.  NDPBs, which used to be called quangos, or quasi-autonomous non-governmental organizations, are not an integral part of a government department and carry out their work at arm's length from ministers, although ministers are ultimately responsible to Parliament for the activities of bodies sponsored by their department. The term includes the four types of NDPB (executive, advisory, tribunal and independent monitoring boards), public corporations, National Health Service (NHS) bodies and public broadcasting authorities. There is a useful list of NDPBs at http://en.wikipedia.org/wiki/QUANGO.
2.  http://www.public-standards.gov.uk/
3.  From Committee on Standards in Public Life (1994) *First Report of the Committee on Standards in Public Life* (the Nolan Report), The Stationery Office, London.
4.  OCPA website and Code of Practice at http://www.ocpa.gov.uk.
5.  *BMJ* (2003) 'Doctors and managers: a problem without a solution?', 22 March, p 609.
6.  Audit Commission Report, 2003, clause 31.
7.  Available from http://www.opm.co.uk/ICGGPS/download_upload/Standard.pdf.
8.  See Appendix 3.

# 18

# IT governance

In the 21st century, IT governance is, within the broader corporate governance context, critical for all organizations. Those without an IT governance strategy face significant risks; those with one perform measurably better.

In today's corporate governance environment, where the value and importance of intellectual assets are significant, boards must be seen to extend the core governance principles – setting strategic aims, providing strategic leadership, overseeing and monitoring the performance of executive management and reporting to shareholders on their stewardship of the organization – to the organization's intellectual capital, information and IT.

A culture of opaqueness is out of line with today's expectation of pro-activity and governance transparency. IT is no longer merely a functional or operational issue. Directors need to be proactive in understanding the strategic importance of, and operational risks in, intellectual capital and information and communications technology.

As younger companies, controlled and managed by people who have grown up with IT and its possibilities, transform the business landscape, so those boards that fail to respond can expect their businesses to be destroyed – and whether the destruction is piece by piece or wholesale is, in the long run, irrelevant.

## IT GOVERNANCE DEFINED

IT governance is a 'framework for the leadership, organizational structures and business processes, standards and compliance to these standards, which ensure that the organization's IT supports and enables the achievement of its strategies and objectives'.[1]

In the future, IT governance may be even more important than corporate governance is today: information and IT are absolutely fundamental to business survival, and organizations that fail to 'direct and control' their IT to best competitive advantage will be left as roadkill on the information superhighway.

The five major drivers of IT governance are:

1.  the search for competitive advantage – in the dynamically changing information economy – through intellectual assets, information and IT;

2.  rapidly evolving governance requirements across the OECD, underpinned by capital market and regulatory convergence;

3.  increasing information- and privacy-related legislation (compliance);

4.  the proliferation of threats to intellectual assets, information and IT;

5.  the need to align technology projects with strategic organizational goals, ensuring that they deliver planned value ('project governance').

# THE INFORMATION ECONOMY AND INTELLECTUAL CAPITAL

The new information, or knowledge, economy is fundamentally different from the old manufacturing one. The globalization of markets, products and resourcing has led to increasingly similar shopping streets selling increasingly similar products throughout the developed world. Over 70 per cent of workers in developed economies are now knowledge, rather than manual, workers – including those factory and farm workers whose work depends on understanding and using information technology. Information networking and telecommunications connectivity make this 'global village' possible – but bring numerous threats and challenges at the same time.

The key characteristics of this global information economy are as follows:

▊  Information and knowledge are not depleting resources to be protected; on the contrary, sharing knowledge drives innovation.

▊  Effects of location and time are diminished – virtual organizations now operate round the clock in virtual marketplaces, so that organizations based on the east coast of the United States can manufacture in China, handle customer support from India and sell globally through a single website.

▌ Laws and taxes are difficult to apply effectively on a national basis, as knowledge quickly shifts to low-tax, low-regulation environments.

▌ Knowledge-enhanced products command price premiums.

▌ Captured knowledge has a greater intrinsic value than 'knowledge on the hoof'.

In a very real sense, knowledge grows as it is shared; more knowledge leads to more innovation, which drives more competition, which in turn drives more globalization.

In the manufacturing economy, an organization's key asset was its productive capability: its machinery, logistical support and distribution equipment, and its stocks of raw materials and finished goods. In the information age, an organization's key asset is its intellectual capital: its human resources, retained knowledge, structural capital and intangible assets. Every organization with a long-term desire to survive and succeed in its chosen market has to focus on preserving, protecting, developing and applying its intellectual capital for the benefit of its shareholders.

Intellectual capital can be valued; in listed companies, for example, it is roughly equivalent to the difference between the market value of the company and its balance sheet net asset value.

Intellectual capital depends, for its productive existence, on information and communication technology: proper IT governance is, therefore, fundamental to both the proper governance and the long-term survival of any 21st-century organization.

# COMPETITIVENESS

IT is neither low-cost nor low-impact. It is investment-intensive. Innovation is common; speed of innovation and deployment can be critical in developing and maintaining competitive advantage. Organizations must respond proactively to change within their markets or see their competitive position eroded and ultimately destroyed. Schumpeter called the process 'Creative Destruction':

[the] process of Creative Destruction is the essential fact about capitalism... every business strategy acquires its true significance

only against the background of that process and with the situation created by it. It must be seen in its role in the perennial gale of creative destruction; it cannot be understood irrespective of it or, in fact, on the hypothesis that there is a perennial lull...[2]

IT on its own and of itself is not, however, necessarily a source of competitive advantage. The way it is used by an organization may be a source of competitive advantage, but in many situations, IT is already commoditized, and organizations have to ensure that their systems and processes are as good as (or no worse than) those of their competitors, in order to ensure they don't fall behind in key performance areas.

IT makes revolutionary business models[3] possible and dramatically transforms the business environment. The challenge of online security only slows – but doesn't halt – the development of online banking and financial and other e-commerce applications.

The internet enables small businesses everywhere to compete with larger ones, globally; digital communication speeds up outsourcing, customer awareness and reputation destruction. Instant messaging, VoIP (Voice over IP), spyware and sequential auto-responders are technologies as disruptive as customer relationship management (CRM), human resource management (HRM) and enterprise resource planning (ERP) systems were in their day. Of course, the internet doesn't replace the need for a real business strategy or for generating a proper economic return for shareholders: it just transforms the environment within which the board has to create and execute strategy.

Risk management, as we saw earlier, has always been a key governance issue. The board's job is strategy and, therefore, strategic risk has always been a board responsibility. The modern corporation's fundamental goal is to create and add value to its business continuously. This means that boards must find an appropriate balance between profit maximization and risk reduction.

Strategic risk can be described as the enterprise-level risk of a negative impact on earnings or capital arising from an organization's future business plans and strategies, improper implementation of decisions, or lack of responsiveness to industry changes. It includes risks associated with plans for entering new businesses, expanding existing services, mergers, acquisitions and divestments, and enhancing the infrastructure.

Two key strategic risks related to information and communications technology are: interruptions to business processes and customer services; and overspending on IT, placing the company at a cost disadvantage to its competitors. Both these risks should be dealt with as part of the strategic risk management process.

In the last few years, the parallel importance of operational risk ('the risk of direct or indirect loss resulting from inadequate or failed internal processes, people and systems or from external events'[4]) has, driven by the Basel 2 process, been recognized.

## Enterprise risk management[5]

Risk assessment has sometimes become a pervasive and invasive concept: a risk assessment must be structured and formal, and nowadays one is expected in almost every context – from a school outing through to a major corporate acquisition. It is certainly a cornerstone of today's corporate governance regimes. In the context of both strategic and operational risk, risk identification and assessment are the first steps that a board should take to controlling the risks facing the organization; the most important step is the development of a risk treatment plan (in which risks are accepted, controlled, eliminated or contracted out) that is appropriate in the context of the company's strategic objectives.

## IT risk management

IT risk management has also now become a hot IT topic. As organizations become increasingly dependent on information technology and intellectual capital assets, the key areas of IT risk are usually seen as:

▌ IT infrastructure and network security – arising from concerns about hackers, terrorists, cyber-criminals, insiders, outsiders, viruses and so on;

▌ data integrity, confidentiality, privacy and compliance – arising from regulatory and market pressure around protecting both personal data (eg data protection legislation) and corporate data (eg fair disclosure regulations), as well as financial and operational data (eg Sarbanes–Oxley);

▌ business continuity – arising from concerns about the capability to continue in business after a natural or human-created disaster;

▌ IT management – arising from concerns about project failure, poor IT operational performance, inadequate IT infrastructure, etc.

These risks all affect more than just the IT organization within the enterprise; their impact is felt across the entire organization, and they must therefore be managed within the enterprise risk management framework. IT governance ensures that IT is fully integrated into the organization and enables the board to govern IT within the context of the overall business model, strategy and risk management framework.

# COMPLIANCE RISK

Information is increasingly subject to legislation. Customers, staff, suppliers, tribunals and law courts all expect organizations to comply proactively with it. There is international, foreign and industry-specific legislation and regulation. All OECD countries have some form of data protection and privacy legislation. National regulations often overlap, are sometimes contradictory and almost all lack implementation guidance or adequate precision. Copyright, digital rights, computer misuse and electronic trading legislation is changing rapidly, and money laundering, proceeds of crime, human rights and freedom of information legislation add to the confusion.

Complex organizations, with diversified or (partially) virtual business models, operating in and across a number of legal jurisdictions, have an even more complex task. While any one regulation (and its related compliance issues) might apply only to a subsidiary national entity, it is the global parent whose reputation might be damaged, and the more failures, the more damage.

Regulatory compliance and risk management appear to go hand in hand. The best companies have always addressed strategic risk from the boardroom; Basel 2 and today's corporate governance regimes increasingly expect risk management to be pervasive throughout the culture of all organizations:

▌ UK Combined Code and Turnbull Guidance. The United Kingdom's Combined Code requires listed companies to review annually 'all material controls, including financial, operational and compliance controls, and risk management systems'.[6] The Turnbull Guidance explicitly requires boards, on an ongoing basis, to identify, assess and deal with significant risks in all areas, including in information and communications processes.[7]

▌ Sarbanes–Oxley. The Sarbanes–Oxley Act of 2002 (SOX) requires US listed companies to assess annually the effectiveness of their internal controls, for the CEO and CFO to certify annually the adequacy of these internal controls, and for the external auditors to attest this. Section 409 requires companies to notify the SEC 'on a rapid and current basis [of] such additional information concerning material changes in the financial condition or operations of the issuer'.

These governance regimes – particularly Sarbanes–Oxley – have substantial IT compliance components.

Authorities are increasingly looking to regulation to force the issue up the corporate agenda.

# INFORMATION RISK

Organizational information is an asset and therefore, by definition, someone outside the organization will want it; if no one wanted it, it wouldn't be an asset. For information to be useful to an organization:

■ it must be available (to those who need to use it);

■ it must be confidential (so that competitors can't use it); and

■ its integrity must be guaranteed (so that it can be relied upon).

Information risk arises from the threats – originating both externally and internally – to the availability, confidentiality and integrity of the organization's information assets.

Headline figures illustrate the cost of security failures: the United Kingdom's National High Tech Crime Unit (NHTCU) reported that 89 per cent of firms interviewed had suffered some form of computer crime in the previous 12 months (up from 83 per cent in the previous year), at a cost of at least £2.4 billion.[8]

Threats to information security are wide-ranging, complex and costly. External threats include:

■ casual criminals (virus writers and hackers);

■ organized crime (virus writers, hackers, spammers, fraudsters, spies and ex-employees); and

■ terrorists (including anarchists).

Securing information against organized crime and cyber-terrorism should be high on corporate agendas.

More information security incidents (involving members of staff, contractors and consultants acting either maliciously or carelessly) originate inside the organization than outside it. White-collar crime is, nowadays, largely computer-based. Barings Bank, Enron, WorldCom and Arthur Andersen were all brought down by insiders.

The indirect costs of information security incidents usually far exceed their direct ones, and the reputational impacts are often even greater.

# PROJECT GOVERNANCE

Organizations continuously upgrade their systems or deploy new systems to improve customer service, reduce cost, improve product or service quality and deliver new products, services and business models. These deployments often involve strategic risk for the organization; they always involve operational risk.

Risk management is a board responsibility and, therefore, project governance – from inception through to deployment – must also be a board responsibility.

IT projects are not always delivered successfully. Authoritative research shows that the majority of projects fail to deliver the benefits that justified commencing the project, and that of those that do, the majority come in late and/or over budget.

Organizations whose IT projects failed usually all deployed recognizable project management methodologies; the reasons for failure were invariably to do with failures of project governance rather than simply of operational management.

Increasingly, shareholders are concerned about project failure. In the past, investment analysts were reluctant to assess IT. Institutional shareholders are now becoming more muscular. Technology is as significant a component of the organization's cost base as its headcount, but usually consumes substantially more capital.

Driven, in part, by the changing corporate governance climate and, in equal part, by the poor record of IT projects, stakeholders and institutional shareholders increasingly seek transparency around IT.

The Standish Group's research on IT project failure found that:

- 16.2 per cent of software projects were completed on time and on budget;

- 31 per cent of projects were cancelled before completion; and

▌ 53 per cent of projects would cost over 189 per cent of their original estimates.[9]

More recent surveys indicate that nothing much has changed.

But it's not only about project failure: 80 per cent of corporate assets today are digital,[10] and, as shareholders and boards focus on the extent to which information and intellectual capital are fundamental to their competitive position and long-term survival, so they recognize the fiduciary nature of their responsibility to shareholders in respect of the organization's information assets and IT.

As they recognize the impact that technology has on business performance (and, consequently, on shareholder value), so they look increasingly for a framework that ensures that IT projects are aligned with commercial objectives and that enables companies to quantify and report in a consistent manner on IT investments.[11]

IT investment decisions (for *or* against) expose an organization to significant risk: strategic, financial, operational and competitive. The pace of change is a significant risk. Project risks must be assessed within the organization's strategic planning and risk management framework for the right decision, one that enhances competitive advantage and delivers measurable value, to be made. Critically, projects need continual oversight; the assumptions on which they were predicated need continual reassessment, and the expected benefits need regular reappraisal.

# WHAT IS IN AN IT GOVERNANCE FRAMEWORK?

An IT governance framework consists, essentially, of a set of principles, a decision-making hierarchy and a tailor-made suite of reporting and monitoring processes.

There are eight key decision areas for designing an IT governance framework:

1.  IT governance principles and decision-making hierarchy. There are two types of principle in this context:

    a.  governance principles, to do with how IT is to be managed in the enterprise, and

    b.  implementation principles, to do with how IT is to be used to achieve the business strategy.

2. The information strategy (which must be derived from the business strategy):

   a. What information do we need, where does it come from and what are we going to do with it?

   b. Out of the information strategy comes the ICT strategy, which is made up of:

      i. application,

      ii. architecture, and

      iii. infrastructure/technology strategies.

3. IT risk management – within the context of the organization's overall risk management framework, risk to information and ICT needs to be treated in line with organization-wide criteria. These criteria should be reflected in the controls developed as part of the IT governance framework and the reporting and monitoring processes.

4. Software applications – how business applications are specified, developed, authorized, acquired and managed.

5. ICT architecture – including the integration and standardization requirements – that will meet the requirements of the information and applications strategy.

6. ICT infrastructure/technology:

   a. How are IT services (including hardware and communications protocols) specified, developed, authorized, acquired and managed?

   b. What services should be outsourced, how, why and to whom?

7. ICT investment and project governance. Given the ICT strategy:

   a. which IT initiatives (including outsourcing initiatives) should be implemented?

   b. how should they be prioritized?

   c. how should they be project-managed?

   d. what returns should be expected?

   e. how should the portfolio of projects be managed?

   f. how should any resultant business change be managed?

8.  Information compliance and security:

    a.  What are the criteria for securing information?

    b.  How do we demonstrate legal/regulatory compliance?

    c.  How should this be measured and demonstrated?

    d.  How is intellectual property protected?

    e.  What audits are required?

# IT STEERING COMMITTEE

IT governance is as much about IT leadership as anything else. The board needs to create a mechanism through which it can provide the business with technology leadership. Technology or IT leadership requires a specific mechanism, in a way that, for instance, neither human resources (HR) nor sales does, for two reasons:

1.  HR, sales, marketing, etc are usually already dealt with effectively as part of the existing board agenda; most board members already understand the issues around sales and marketing, and the people involved in making sales happen already get a great deal of informed attention. The organization almost certainly already has well-developed governance frameworks for these key activities. No additional benefits would accrue to the organization through the creation of additional leadership mechanisms for these activities.

2.  IT, in contrast, is not as well understood at board level, and there are usually no established IT governance frameworks inside organizations. It is not well understood, but it is critical: on average, investment in IT represents more than 50 per cent of every organization's annual capital investment and, typically, more than 30 per cent of its cost base is in IT – for most businesses, the direct cost of IT operations is now second only to staffing as an expense item. There is, in other words, a gap between the importance of IT and the understanding of IT: an IT governance framework closes that gap, providing all those with a limited understanding of IT in the enterprise with a framework within which they can improve their understanding to a level appropriate for this critical contributor to their competitive position.

The board-level IT steering or strategy committee has a number of functions, some of which (depending on the size, structure and complexity of the organization) may be dealt with through subcommittees.

This committee takes the lead in dealing with IT governance principles (including the decision-making hierarchy), strategy and risk treatment criteria. The board also has a key monitoring and oversight role across the whole of IT, and particularly in respect of project governance. This monitoring component means that the board IT committee has similarities to the audit committee and, given the extent to which IT governance issues impinge on audit issues (particularly around internal control, eg Sarbanes–Oxley), there is some sense in having a number of members of each committee in common.

They are not the same committees, though. In some organizations the monitoring component of the IT governance framework will be included in the agenda of the audit committee, in order to ensure a clear segregation between those responsible for determining the ICT strategy of the organization and approving investment, and those responsible for monitoring and overseeing the appropriateness and effectiveness of those decisions.

## Composition of the IT steering committee

The composition of the board steering committee should be straightforward. The chair should be selected on exactly the same basis, following the same rules, as the chair of the audit committee. There should be a majority of independent directors on the committee, and key executives should be invited to attend: the CEO, the CFO and the CIO (or equivalent) would be included as a minimum. In some organizations, it would be appropriate to include the chief compliance officer (CCO) as well.

The other key business heads in the organization (whether production, procurement, retail, sales, marketing, etc depends on the sector, the organization and the existing management structure) – the ones who would be included in any business strategy committee – should be included in the IT steering committee.

The CIO's position and level of accountability should be clear. The CIO should be on the same level, and have the same status, as the CFO and the other functional heads (eg sales, marketing, etc), with direct responsibility for managing the IT operations and personal accountability for the success of organizational IT activity.

1.  The IT steering committee needs at least one independent director who has the right mix of business and IT experience and sufficient gravitas to lead the board's IT governance efforts.

2.  All the other non-executive directors should be prepared and determined to question every aspect of IT planning and activity.

3.  The executive – particularly the CIO and the IT management – should be banned from using IT jargon and forced to express everything they have to say about IT in a format that focuses on comprehensible (to the non-IT specialist) opportunities, issues, risks or plans.

4.  The IT steering committee should have access to external, professional advice on this as on other matters. Employ outside experts (strategic IT consultants) as board advisers with the specific brief of confirming that what the board has been told is accurate, complete and true, and if not, what has been left out.

# ENTERPRISE IT ARCHITECTURE COMMITTEE

A critical component of a useful IT governance framework is the enterprise IT architecture. The determination of this architecture can only take place in the context of the business and information strategies, in line with the key IT implementation principles and taking the security, compliance and risk treatment criteria into account.

The enterprise IT architecture is a set of organizing principles that determine the way in which the organization's information and communications technology will interact with its operating systems, applications and data.

The architecture should (for instance, if the key principles adopted allow it) ensure technical integration, minimizing inter-system hand-offs (which is where significant cost and risk reside) and allowing the IT organization to respond cost-effectively to businesses needs.

The ongoing role of this committee is to ensure that all ICT deployments (including outsourcing proposals) are in line with it, fiercely warding off attempts to deploy non-standard hardware or systems – unless the architecture itself is adapted, taking into account the ramifications for existing installations, future upgrades and current projects.

This committee might, in larger organizations, be led by a chief architect, who would also be responsible for the formalization and communication across the organization of the architecture.

Key members of the committee, alongside business delegates who understand the organizational architecture, would include senior managers with expertise in systems, data, security and infrastructure. The organizational risk manager should also be involved with this committee.

# IT AUDIT

We covered IT audit earlier, in Chapter 14. An area in which most organizations are inadequate, where IT is concerned, is oversight. 'Oversight' must include oversight by the board and must cover more than internal financial controls. Every board needs to empower either the IT committee or the audit committee to deal with IT oversight.

An IT audit plan, just like a financial audit plan, needs to reflect the organization's key risk areas. It must review regulatory compliance, information security, IT project progress and technical implementation, as well as the skills and competences of the specialized staff employed in the organization.

Its objective is to provide the outside directors with real, technical assurance that the IT implementation principles and the governance framework are being applied, and to identify any areas of non-conformance that need to be drawn to the attention of directors.

Use qualified IT auditors for this work, and insist that they work within your organization's risk and IT governance framework. Pay no attention to non-conformance reports that are based on anything other than your own framework.

# NOTES

1.  Alan Calder (2005) *IT Governance: Guidelines for directors*, IT Governance Publishing, Ely, www.itgovernance.co.uk/products/19.
2.  Joseph A Schumpeter (1962) *Capitalism, Socialism and Democracy*, 3rd edn, Harper Perennial, London.
3.  The term 'business model' 'seems to refer to a loose conception of how a company does business and generates revenue. Yet simply having a business model is an exceedingly low bar to set for building a company. Generating revenue is a far cry from creating economic value, and no business model can be evaluated independently of industry structure. The business model approach to management becomes an invitation for faulty thinking and self-delusion.' Michael E Porter (2001) 'Strategy and the internet', *Harvard Business Review*, March.
4.  'Operational risk', a consultative document from the Basel Committee on Banking Supervision, published in January 2001.
5.  Discussed at greater length in Chapter 12.
6.  Combined Code on Corporate Governance, Section C.2.1.
7.  Turnbull Guidance, para 20.

8.   'Hi-tech crime: the impact on UK business 2005', survey conducted by NOP for the United Kingdom's NHTCU.
9.   Standish Group (1994) 'The chaos report'.
10.  Testimony of Jody R Westby, PwC Managing Director, to the House of Congress Committee on Government Reform, September 2004.
11.  HP IT Governance Roundtable, 24 October 2002.

# 19

# Corporate social responsibility

I quoted Sir Adrian Cadbury in the Introduction to this book: 'Corporations work within a governance framework which is set first by the law and then by regulations emanating from the regulatory bodies to which they are subject. In addition, publicly quoted companies are subject to their shareholders in general meeting and all companies to the forces of public opinion.'[1]

Corporate social responsibility (CSR) is the leading example of how the governance of companies has to conform, sooner or later, to public opinion. CSR does not form part of either the statutory or the non-statutory corporate governance framework. There are a number of versions of CSR, and companies have many motives – not all of them entirely transparent – in pursuing CSR agendas. This chapter will provide no more than the most basic of introductions to an issue that is, today, outside the formal corporate governance agenda. It is likely to find itself increasingly on the corporate governance agenda and, therefore, directors and practitioners should ensure that they adequately inform themselves on this subject.

Corporate social responsibility is described in Wikipedia as:

> a concept which encourages organizations to consider the interests of society by taking responsibility for the impact of the organization's activities on customers, employees, shareholders, communities and the environment in all aspects of its operations. This obligation is seen to extend beyond the statutory obligation to comply with legislation and sees organizations voluntarily taking further steps to improve the quality of life for employees and their families as well as for the local community and society at large.

One apparently widely quoted definition by the World Business Council for Sustainable Development states that 'Corporate Social Responsibility is the continuing commitment by business to behave ethically and contribute to economic development while improving the quality of life of the workforce and their families as well as of the local community and society at large.'[2]

# OECD GUIDELINES

In 2001, the OECD published a set of guidelines for multinational organizations.[3]

The purpose of these guidelines was described, in their preface, as follows:

> The OECD Guidelines for Multinational Enterprises (the Guidelines) are recommendations addressed by governments to multinational enterprises. They provide voluntary principles and standards for responsible business conduct consistent with applicable laws. The Guidelines aim to ensure that the operations of these enterprises are in harmony with government policies, to strengthen the basis of mutual confidence between enterprises and the societies in which they operate, to help improve the foreign investment climate and to enhance the contribution to sustainable development made by multinational enterprises. The Guidelines are part of the OECD Declaration on International Investment and Multinational Enterprises the other elements of which relate to national treatment, conflicting requirements on enterprises, and international investment incentives and disincentives.

# UK APPROACH TO CSR

The UK government has an interest in CSR. In *Corporate Social Responsibility: A government update*,[4] the government describes its CSR vision as: 'seeing UK businesses taking account of their economic, social and environmental impacts, and acting to address the key sustainable development challenges based on their core competences wherever they operate – locally, regionally and internationally'. The report should be downloaded and read, as it provides a clear picture of where the government is going on this subject.

# CSR REPORTING STANDARDS

There are a number of recognized standards against which companies can report their CSR activity. The first is SA8000. SA8000 is a global social accountability standard for decent working conditions, developed and overseen by Social Accountability International (SAI).[5] SAI's mission is 'to promote human rights for workers around the world'.

Detailed guidance for implementing, or auditing, to SA8000 are available from its website. SAI offers training in SA8000 and other workplace standards to managers, workers and auditors. It also operates an accreditation agency that licenses and oversees auditing organizations to award certification to employers that comply with SA8000.

SA8000 covers the following areas of accountability:

▌ child labour;

▌ forced labour;

▌ workplace safety and health;

▌ the right to organize;

▌ discrimination;

▌ workplace discipline;

▌ working hours;

▌ wages;

▌ management systems for human resources.

The second widely recognized framework is that of the Global Reporting Initiative, which is called 'a common framework for sustainability reporting' and which is more widely focused on sustainability than simply on human rights in supply chains.

The Global Reporting Initiative's (GRI) vision is that reporting on economic, environmental, and social performance by all organizations becomes as routine and comparable as financial reporting. GRI accomplishes this vision by developing, continually improving, and building capacity around the use of its Sustainability Reporting Framework.

An international network of thousands from business, civil society, labor, and professional institutions create the content of the

Reporting Framework in a consensus-seeking process.[6]

GRI describes sustainability reporting as follows:

> Sustainability reporting is the practice of measuring, disclosing, and being accountable to internal and external stakeholders for organizational performance towards the goal of sustainable development. 'Sustainability reporting' is a broad term considered synonymous with others used to describe reporting on economic, environmental, and social impacts (eg, triple bottom line, corporate responsibility reporting, etc).
>
> A sustainability report should provide a balanced and reasonable representation of the sustainability performance of a reporting organization – including both positive and negative contributions.
>
> Sustainability reports based on the GRI Reporting Framework disclose outcomes and results that occurred within the reporting period in the context of the organization's commitments, strategy, and management approach. Reports can be used for the following purposes, among others:

- **Benchmarking** and assessing sustainability performance with respect to laws, norms, codes, performance standards, and voluntary initiatives;

- **Demonstrating** how the organization influences and is influenced by expectations about sustainable development; and

- **Comparing** performance within an organization and between different organizations over time.[7]

The GRI Guidelines (the third generation, or G3, was launched in 2006) were designed to provide universal guidance for reporting on sustainability performance. This means they are applicable to small companies, large multinationals, public sector organizations, NGOs and other types of organizations from all around the world.

# NOTES

1.   Sir Adrian Cadbury (1998) 'The future of governance: the rules of the game', *Journal of General Management*, **24** (1), Autumn.

2.  World Business Council for Sustainable Development (1999) *CSR: Meeting changing expectations*, WBCSD Publications, Geneva.
3.  The OECD Guidelines for Multinational Enterprises can be downloaded from http://www.oecd.org/document/28/0,3343,en_2649_34889_2397532_1_1_1_1,00.html.
4.  Available from http://www.csr.gov.uk/pdf/dti_csr_final.pdf.
5.  See their website: http://www.sa-intl.org/.
6.  Quote from the front page of the GRI website: http://www.global reporting.org/Home.
7.  Global Reporting Initiative (2002) *Sustainability Reporting Guidelines*, GRI, Boston, MA.

# Appendix 1

# Table of contents: the Companies Act 2006

This table of contents is reproduced from the Companies Act 2006, and is provided to help the reader identify precisely where specific issues of the statutory corporate governance framework can be found. This table of contents has been reproduced subject to Crown Copyright, and a full copy of the Act itself can be downloaded from http://www.opsi.gov.uk/ACTS/acts2006/ukpga_20060046_en.pdf.

## PART 1: GENERAL INTRODUCTORY PROVISIONS

### Companies and Companies Acts

### Types of company

# PART 2: COMPANY FORMATION

## *General*

## *Requirements for registration*

# PART 3: A COMPANY'S CONSTITUTION

## Chapter 1: Introductory

## Chapter 2: Articles of association

### *General*

### *Alteration of articles*

## Supplementary

## Chapter 3: Resolutions and agreements affecting a company's constitution

## Chapter 4: Miscellaneous and supplementary provisions

### Statement of company's objects

### Supplementary provisions

# PART 4: A COMPANY'S CAPACITY AND RELATED MATTERS

### Capacity of company and power of directors to bind it

### Formalities of doing business under the law of England and Wales or Northern Ireland

# PART 5: A COMPANY'S NAME

## Chapter 1: General requirements

### *Prohibited names*

### *Permitted characters etc*

## Chapter 2: Indications of company type or legal form

### *Required indications for limited companies*

# PART 6: A COMPANY'S REGISTERED OFFICE

## General

## Welsh companies

# PART 7: RE-REGISTRATION AS A MEANS OF ALTERING A COMPANY'S STATUS

## Introductory

## Private company becoming public

## Public company becoming private

## Private limited company becoming unlimited

## Chapter 3: Overseas branch registers

## Chapter 4: Prohibition on subsidiary being member of its holding company

### *General prohibition*

### *Subsidiary acting as personal representative or trustee*

### *Subsidiary acting as dealer in securities*

### *Supplementary*

# PART 9: EXERCISE OF MEMBERS' RIGHTS

## *Effect of provisions in company's articles*

## *Information rights*

## *Exercise of rights where shares held on behalf of others*

# PART 10: A COMPANY'S DIRECTORS

## Chapter 1: Appointment and removal of directors

### *Requirement to have directors*

### *Appointment*

## *Register of directors, etc*

## *Removal*

# Chapter 2: General duties of directors

## *Introductory*

## *The general duties*

## *Supplementary provisions*

# Chapter 3: Declaration of interest in existing transaction or arrangement

# Chapter 4: Transactions with directors requiring approval of members

## Supplementary

## Chapter 5: Directors' service contracts

## Chapter 6: Contracts with sole members who are directors

## Chapter 7: Directors' liabilities

## Provision protecting directors from liability

# PART 11: DERIVATIVE CLAIMS AND PROCEEDINGS BY MEMBERS

## Chapter 1: Derivative claims in England and Wales or Northern Ireland

## Chapter 2: Derivative proceedings in Scotland

# PART 12: COMPANY SECRETARIES

*Private companies*

*Public companies*

*Provisions applying to private companies with a secretary and to public companies*

# PART 13: RESOLUTIONS AND MEETINGS

## Chapter 1: General provisions about resolutions

## Chapter 2: Written resolutions

### *General provisions about written resolutions*

### *Circulation of written resolutions*

### *Agreeing to written resolutions*

### *Supplementary*

## Chapter 3: Resolutions at meetings

### *General provisions about resolutions at meetings*

## Calling meetings

## Notice of meetings

## Members' statements

## Procedure at meetings

## Proxies

## *Adjourned meetings*

## *Electronic communications*

## *Application to class meetings*

## Chapter 4: Public companies: additional requirements for AGMs

## Chapter 5: Additional requirements for quoted companies

### *Website publication of poll results*

### *Independent report on poll*

# PART 14: CONTROL OF POLITICAL DONATIONS AND EXPENDITURE

# PART 15: ACCOUNTS AND REPORTS

## Chapter 1: Introduction

*General*

## Chapter 2: Accounting records

# Chapter 3: A company's financial year

# Chapter 4: Annual accounts

## General

## Individual accounts

## Group accounts: small companies

## Group accounts: other companies

## Group accounts: general

## Information to be given in notes to the accounts

*Right of member or debenture holder to demand copies of accounts and reports*

*Requirements in connection with publication of accounts and reports*

## Chapter 8: Public companies: laying of accounts and reports before general meeting

## Chapter 9: Quoted companies: members' approval of directors' remuneration report

## Chapter 10: Filing of accounts and reports

*Duty to file accounts and reports*

*Filing obligations of different descriptions of company*

## *Requirements where abbreviated accounts delivered*

## *Failure to file accounts and reports*

# Chapter 11: Revision of defective accounts and reports

## *Voluntary revision*

## *Secretary of State's notice*

## *Application to court*

## *Power of authorised person to require documents etc*

# Chapter 12: Supplementary provisions

## *Liability for false or misleading statements in reports*

## *Accounting and reporting standards*

## Companies qualifying as medium-sized

## General power to make further provision about accounts and reports

## Other supplementary provisions

# PART 16: AUDIT

## Chapter 1: Requirement for audited accounts

### Requirement for audited accounts

### Exemption from audit: small companies

### Exemption from audit: dormant companies

### Companies subject to public sector audit

## General power of amendment by regulations

# Chapter 2: Appointment of auditors

## Private companies

## Public companies

## General provisions

# Chapter 3: Functions of auditor

## Auditor's report

## Duties and rights of auditors

## *Signature of auditor's report*

## *Offences in connection with auditor's report*

# Chapter 4: Removal, resignation, etc of auditors

## *Removal of auditor*

## *Failure to re-appoint auditor*

## *Resignation of auditor*

## *Statement by auditor on ceasing to hold office*

*Supplementary*

## Chapter 5: Quoted companies: right of members to raise audit concerns at accounts meeting

## Chapter 6: Auditors' liability

*Voidness of provisions protecting auditors from liability*

*Indemnity for costs of defending proceedings*

*Liability limitation agreements*

## Chapter 7: Supplementary provisions

# PART 17: A COMPANY'S SHARE CAPITAL

## Chapter 1: Shares and share capital of a company

*Shares*

## Chapter 3: Allotment of equity securities: existing shareholders' right of pre-emption

# Chapter 4: Public companies: allotment where issue not fully subscribed

# Chapter 5: Payment for shares

## General rules

## Additional rules for public companies

## Supplementary provisions

# Chapter 6: Public companies: independent valuation of non-cash consideration

## Non-cash consideration for shares

## Transfer of non-cash asset in initial period

## Supplementary provisions

# Chapter 7: Share premiums

## The share premium account

## Relief from requirements as to share premiums

## Supplementary provisions

# Chapter 8: Alteration of share capital

## How share capital may be altered

## **Chapter 9: Classes of share and class rights**

### *Introductory*

### *Variation of class rights*

### *Matters to be notified to the registrar*

## Chapter 10: Reduction of share capital

*Introductory*

*Private companies: reduction of capital supported by solvency statement*

*Reduction of capital confirmed by the court*

*Public company reducing capital below authorised minimum*

*Effect of reduction of capital*

## Chapter 11: Miscellaneous and supplementary provisions

# PART 18: ACQUISITION BY LIMITED COMPANY OF ITS OWN SHARES

## Chapter 1: General provisions

### *Introductory*

### *Shares held by company's nominee*

### *Shares held by or for public company*

### *Charges of public company on own shares*

### *Supplementary provisions*

## Chapter 2: Financial assistance for purchase of own shares

*Introductory*

*Circumstances in which financial assistance prohibited*

*Exceptions from prohibition*

*Supplementary*

## Chapter 3: Redeemable shares

## Chapter 4: Purchase of own shares

*General provisions*

*Authority for purchase of own shares*

## Chapter 5: Redemption or purchase by private company out of capital

### Introductory

### The permissible capital payment

### Requirements for payment out of capital

# PART 20: PRIVATE AND PUBLIC COMPANIES

## Chapter 1: Prohibition of public offers by private companies

## Chapter 2: Minimum share capital requirement for public companies

# PART 21: CERTIFICATION AND TRANSFER OF SECURITIES

## Chapter 1: Certification and transfer of securities: general

### Share certificates

### Issue of certificates etc on allotment

### Transfer of securities

### Issue of certificates etc on transfer

### Issue of certificates etc on allotment or transfer to financial institution

### Share warrants

## Orders imposing restrictions on shares

## Power of members to require company to act

## Register of interests disclosed

## Meaning of interest in shares

## Other supplementary provisions

# PART 23: DISTRIBUTIONS

## Chapter 1: Restrictions on when distributions may be made

### Introductory

### General rules

### Distributions by investment companies

## Chapter 2: Justification of distribution by reference to accounts

### Justification of distribution by reference to accounts

### Requirements applicable in relation to relevant accounts

### Application of provisions to successive distributions etc

## Chapter 3: Supplementary provisions

*Accounting matters*

*Distributions in kind*

*Consequences of unlawful distribution*

*Other matters*

# PART 24: A COMPANY'S ANNUAL RETURN

# PART 25: COMPANY CHARGES

## Chapter 1: Companies registered in England and Wales or in Northern Ireland

### Requirement to register company charges

### Special rules about debentures

### Charges in other jurisdictions

### Orders charging land: Northern Ireland

### The register of charges

### Avoidance of certain charges

### Companies' records and registers

## Chapter 2: Companies registered in Scotland

### Charges requiring registration

### Special rules about debentures

### Charges on property outside the United Kingdom

### The register of charges

### Avoidance of certain charges

### Companies' records and registers

## Chapter 3: Powers of the Secretary of State

# PART 26: ARRANGEMENTS AND RECONSTRUCTIONS

# PART 27: MERGERS AND DIVISIONS OF PUBLIC COMPANIES

## Chapter 1: Introductory

## Chapter 2: Merger

# Chapter 2: Impediments to takeovers

## *Opting in and opting out*

## *Consequences of opting in*

## *Supplementary*

# Chapter 3: 'Squeeze-out' and 'sell-out'

## *Takeover offers*

## *'Squeeze-out'*

## *'Sell-out'*

## *Supplementary*

## *Interpretation*

### Chapter 4: Amendments to Part 7 of the Companies Act 1985

# PART 29: FRAUDULENT TRADING

# PART 30: PROTECTION OF MEMBERS AGAINST UNFAIR PREJUDICE

## *Main provisions*

## *Supplementary provisions*

# PART 31: DISSOLUTION AND RESTORATION TO THE REGISTER

## Chapter 1: Striking off

### *Registrar's power to strike off defunct company*

## Voluntary striking off

# Chapter 2: Property of dissolved company

## Property vesting as bona vacantia

## Effect of Crown disclaimer: England and Wales and Northern Ireland

## Effect of Crown disclaimer: Scotland

## Supplementary provisions

## Certificates of incorporation

## Registered numbers

## Delivery of documents to the registrar

## Requirements for proper delivery

## Public notice of receipt of certain documents

## The register

## Inspection etc of the register

# PART 36: OFFENCES UNDER THE COMPANIES ACTS

## *Liability of officer in default*

## *Offences under the Companies Act 1985*

## *General provisions*

## *Production and inspection of documents*

## *Supplementary*

# PART 37: COMPANIES: SUPPLEMENTARY PROVISIONS

# PART 38: COMPANIES: INTERPRETATION

# PART 39: COMPANIES: MINOR AMENDMENTS

# PART 40: COMPANY DIRECTORS: FOREIGN DISQUALIFICATION ETC

## *Introductory*

## *Power to disqualify*

## *Power to make persons liable for company's debts*

## *Power to require statements to be sent to the registrar of companies*

# PART 41: BUSINESS NAMES

## Chapter 1: Restricted or prohibited names

### *Introductory*

### *Sensitive words or expressions*

## Chapter 2: Disclosure required in case of individual or partnership

### Introductory

### Disclosure requirements

### Consequences of failure to make required disclosure

## Chapter 3: Supplementary

# PART 42: STATUTORY AUDITORS

## Chapter 1: Introductory

## Chapter 2: Individuals and firms

*Eligibility for appointment*

*Independence requirement*

*Effect of appointment of a partnership*

*Supervisory bodies*

*Professional qualifications*

*Information*

*Enforcement*

## Chapter 3: Auditors General

# Chapter 4: The register of auditors etc

# Chapter 5: Registered third country auditors

## Introductory

## Duties

## Information

## Enforcement

# Chapter 6: Supplementary and general

## Power to require second company audit

## False and misleading statements

## Fees

## Delegation of Secretary of State's functions

# PART 43: TRANSPARENCY OBLIGATIONS AND RELATED MATTERS

## Introductory

## Transparency obligations

# PART 46: GENERAL SUPPLEMENTARY PROVISIONS

# PART 47: FINAL PROVISIONS

# Appendix 2

# The Combined Code on Corporate Governance

The Financial Reporting Council required an unacceptably high fee payment to license the reproduction here of the Combined Code on Corporate Governance.

Anyone can, however, download the Combined Code and its associated documents free of charge as follows:

- A copy of the 2006 version of the Combined Code can be downloaded from http://www.frc.org.uk/documents/pagemanager/frc/Combined%20Code%20June%202006.pdf.
- The Turnbull Guidance is available from http://www.frc.org.uk/corporate/internalcontrol.cfm.
- The October 2005 version of the Smith Guidance is available from http://www.frc.org.uk/documents/pagemanager/frc/Smith%20Report%202005.pdf.
- The January 2003 version of the Higgs Report (published by the FRC in June 2006) is available from http://www.frc.org.uk/documents/pagemanager/frc/Suggestions%20for%20good%20practice%20from%20the%20Higgs%20Report%20June%202006.pdf.

# Appendix 3

# Corporate Governance Guidelines for AIM Companies

This appendix contains the central code of practice from the QCA's Corporate Governance Guidelines for AIM Companies.[1] It does not contain the Appendices to the Code (which are similar in content to other material in this book or elsewhere in these appendices), nor does it include those sections of the QCA booklet that provide additional guidance on how the AIM Code should be applied; for the full value of the QCA Code, readers should obtain a copy of the full AIM Code booklet directly from the QCA.[2]

## Purpose of corporate governance

The purpose of good corporate governance is to ensure that the company is managed in an efficient, effective and entrepreneurial manner for the benefit of all shareholders over the longer term.

## What features of corporate governance achieve this?

A communication mechanism should exist between board and shareholders so that shareholders understand the constraints on the company.

## Code of best practice for AIM companies

### Matters reserved for the board

There should be a formal schedule of matters specifically reserved for the board's decision (and a specimen list of these is set out in Appendix A [of the QCA Code]).

*Timely information*

The board should be supplied in a timely manner with information (including regular management financial information) in a form and of a quality appropriate to enable it to discharge its duties.

## Internal controls review

The board should, at least annually, conduct a review of the effectiveness of the group's system of internal controls and should report to shareholders that they have done so.

The review should cover all material controls, including financial, operational and compliance controls and risk management systems.

*Chairman and chief executive*

The roles of chairman and chief executive should not be exercised by the same individual or there should be a clear explanation of how other board procedures provide protection against the risks of concentration of power within the company.

*Independent non-executive directors*

A company should have at least two independent non-executive directors (one of whom may be the chairman) and the board should not be dominated by one person or group of people. A list of factors which might impair a director's independence is set out in Appendix B [of the QCA Code].

*Re-election*

All directors should be submitted for re-election at regular intervals, subject to continued satisfactory performance.

The board should ensure planned and progressive refreshing of the board.

*Audit committee*

The board should establish an audit committee of at least two members, who should all be independent non-executive directors. The main roles and responsibilities of the audit committee (which should be set out in formal terms of reference for the Committee) are set out in Appendix C [of the QCA Code].

*Remuneration committee*

The board should establish a remuneration committee of at least two members, who should all be independent non-executive directors. A summary of the duties of the committee is set out in Appendix D [of the QCA Code].

*Nomination committee*
Recommendations for appointments to the board should be made by a nomination committee (or the board as a whole) and should be made after due evaluation. A summary of the duties of the committee are set out in Appendix E [of the QCA Code].

*Dialogue with shareholders*
There should be a dialogue with shareholders based on the mutual understanding of objectives. The board as a whole has responsibility for ensuring that a satisfactory dialogue with shareholders takes place.

*A Corporate Governance statement on the company's web site*
Companies should publish a Corporate Governance statement annually that describes how they achieve good governance. We recommend that this report is published on the company's web site (which would also be an appropriate place to make available for inspection the items required to be on display as set out below). It could, alternatively, be published in the annual report and accounts. Where the report is published on the company's web site, the Directors' Report should identify where this information can be found and confirm the (recent) date at which it was reviewed and updated.

*Applying the QCA Guidelines*
It is anticipated that all AIM companies will wish to follow good govern-ance and should be able to apply all of the QCA Guidelines set out in this Code.

The Corporate Governance statement should, at a minimum, describe how each of the QCA Guidelines is put into practice by the company and also describe any additional corporate governance standards and procedures that the company applies beyond this basic level.

**Reporting corporate governance**
It is anticipated that a company should be able to (and will) apply all of the QCA Guidelines. Where this is not the case, the statement should describe how the features of good governance are being achieved.

*Basic disclosures*
As well as explaining how the company achieves good governance, the annual report should also include the following 'Basic Disclosures':

- a statement of how the board operates, including a high level statement of which types of decisions are to be taken by the board and which are to be delegated to management;
- the identity of the chairman, the deputy chairman (where there is one), the chief executive, the senior independent director and the chairmen and members of the nomination, audit and remuneration committees;

- the identity of those directors the board considers to be independent and the reasons why it has determined a director to be independent notwithstanding factors which may appear to impair that status. A list of factors which might impair a director's independence is set out in Appendix B [of the QCA Code];
- the board should describe any performance evaluation procedures it applies;
- the names of directors, accompanied by sufficient biographical details (with any other relevant information) to enable shareholders to take an informed decision on the balance of the board and the re-election of certain of them;
- the number of meetings of the board (normally monthly) and of the Committees and individual directors' attendance at them;
- an explanation of the directors' responsibility for preparing the accounts and a statement by the auditors about their reporting responsibilities;
- a statement by the directors that the business is a going concern, with supporting assumptions or qualifications as necessary;
- an explanation to shareholders of how, if the auditor provides significant non-audit services, auditor objectivity and independence is safeguarded.

*Available for inspection*

The following items should be available for inspection on the company's web site or by shareholders on request:

- the terms and conditions of appointment of non-executive directors should be made available for inspection.
- the audit committee should make available its terms of reference, explaining its role and the authority delegated to it by the board.
- the remuneration committee should make available its terms of reference, explaining its role and the authority delegated to it by the board.
- the nomination committee should make available its terms of reference, explaining its role and the authority delegated to it by the board, or the board should explain its processes where it acts as the nomination committee.

# NOTES

1. Reproduced with the permission of the Quoted Companies Alliance, which owns the copyright in this Code and to which any copyright enquiries should be addressed. 'While all reasonable care has been taken in the preparation of this publication, no responsibility or liability is accepted by the authors, QCA, for any errors, omissions or mis-statements it may contain, or for any loss or damage howsoever occasioned, to any person relying on any statement in, or omission from, this publication.'
2. www.quotedcompaniesalliance.co.uk

# Appendix 4

# Summary of the Nolan Committee's First Report on Standards in Public Life

'At the request of the Prime Minister, the Nolan Committee spent six months inquiring into standards in British public life. It concentrated on Members of Parliament, Ministers and Civil Servants, executive Quangos and NHS bodies.'

This summary of the Nolan Committee's report concentrates on the general principles and those that are relevant to organizational and corporate governance. Much of the original report deals with Members of Parliament, ministers and civil servants and, as this is not directly relevant to the subject of this book, it has been omitted from this summary.

It should be noted that the Nolan Committee (originally established in 1994) has now become the Committee on Standards in Public Life.[1]

## The Seven Principles of Public Life

*Selflessness*
Holders of public office should take decisions solely in terms of the public interest. They should not do so in order to gain financial or other material benefits for themselves, their family, or their friends.

*Integrity*
Holders of public office should not place themselves under any financial or other obligation to outside individuals or organisations that might influence them in the performance of their official duties.

*Objectivity*
In carrying out public business, including making public appointments, awarding contracts, or recommending individuals for rewards and benefits, holders of public office should make choices on merit.

*Accountability*
Holders of public office are accountable for their decisions and actions to the public and must submit themselves to whatever scrutiny is appropriate to their office.

*Openness*
Holders of public office should be as open as possible about all the decisions and actions that they take. They should give reasons for their decisions and restrict information only when the wider public interest clearly demands.

*Honesty*
Holders of public office have a duty to declare any private interests relating to their public duties and to take steps to resolve any conflicts arising in a way that protects the public interest.

*Leadership*
Holders of public office should promote and support these principles by leadership and example.

These principles apply to all aspects of public life. The Committee set them out for the benefit of all who serve the public in any way.

## General recommendations

*Codes of Conduct*
All public bodies should draw up Codes of Conduct incorporating the Principles of Public Life.

*Independent Scrutiny*
Internal systems for maintaining standards should be supported by independent scrutiny.

*Education*
More needs to be done to promote and reinforce standards of conduct in public bodies, in particular through guidance and training, including induction training.

In respect of quangos (executive NDPBs and NHS bodies), the Nolan Report said:

Executive Non-Departmental Public Bodies (NDPBs) and National Health Service bodies are public bodies with executive powers whose Boards are appointed by Ministers. They have almost 9000 Board Members and spend some £40bn a year.

There is much public concern about appointments to Quango Boards, and a widespread belief that these are not always made on merit. The Government has committed itself publicly to making all appointments on merit.

While individual posts should always be filled purely on merit, it is important that the overall composition of boards should represent an appropriate mix of relevant skills and background. This range should be clearly and publicly set out in job specifications.

Ministers should continue to make board appointments, but an independent Public Appointments Commissioner should be appointed to regulate, monitor and report on the public appointments process.

The Government is already taking steps to develop best practice and to ensure that the widest range of candidates is secured. In future the Commissioner should recommend best practice and Departments should have to justify any departures from it.

Formal and impartial assessment of candidates is essential. The advisory panels being introduced in the NHS should become universal, and they should all include an independent element. All candidates whom Ministers consider for all appointments should have been approved as suitable by an advisory panel.

Following recent scandals, much has been done to improve and standardise arrangements to secure high standards of conduct in NDPBs. This process needs to continue. All NDPBs and NHS bodies should have codes of conduct, in line with the principles which apply to all public bodies, for board members and staff.

There remain differences in the legal framework governing standards of conduct in NDPBs, NHS bodies and local authorities. The Government needs to review this area and consider whether greater consistency can be achieved.

Further steps are needed to safeguard propriety both internally and externally. Internally, the Accounting Officer's responsibility for propriety as well as financial matters needs to be emphasised, and better confidential avenues are needed for investigation of staff concern about propriety.

Externally, the role of auditors in propriety matters needs to be emphasised. Audit arrangements should be reviewed to ensure that best practice applies to all bodies.

# RECOMMENDATIONS

The Nolan Committee then went on to make some specific recommendations. Those that relate to quangos are set out below, and are discussed in more detail in the report itself.

*Appointments*
33.   The ultimate responsibility for appointments should remain with Ministers.

34.    All public appointments should be governed by the overriding principle of appointment on merit.

35.    Selection on merit should take account of the need to appoint boards which include a balance of skills and backgrounds. The basis on which members are appointed and how they are expected to fulfil their role should be explicit. The range of skills and background which are sought should be clearly specified.

36.    All appointments to executive NDPBs or NHS bodies should be made after advice from a panel or committee which includes an independent element.

37.    Each panel or committee should have at least one independent member and independent members should normally account for at least a third of membership.

38.    A new independent Commissioner for Public Appointments should be appointed, who may be one of the Civil Service Commissioners.

39.    The Public Appointments Commissioner should monitor, regulate and approve departmental appointments procedures.

40.    The Public Appointments Commissioner should publish an annual report on the operation of the public appointments system.

41.    The Public Appointments Unit should be taken out of the Cabinet Office and placed under the control of the Public Appointments Commissioner.

42.    All Secretaries of State should report annually on the public appointments made by their departments.

43.    Candidates for appointment should be required to declare any significant political activity (including office-holding, public speaking and candidature for election) which they have undertaken in the last five years.

44.    The Public Appointments Commissioner should draw up a code of practice for public appointments procedures. Reasons for departures from the code on grounds of 'proportionality' should be documented and capable of review.

*Propriety*

45.    A review should be undertaken by the Government with a view to producing a more consistent legal framework governing propriety and accountability in public bodies, including executive NDPBs, NHS bodies and local government. This should involve all relevant departments and be co-ordinated by the Cabinet Office and the Treasury.

46.    The adoption of a code of conduct for board members should be made mandatory for each executive NDPB and NHS body.

47.    It should be mandatory for the board of each executive NDPB and NHS body to adopt a code of conduct for their staff.

48.    Board members and staff of all executive NDPBs and NHS bodies

should be required on appointment to undertake to uphold and abide by the relevant code, and compliance should be a condition of appointment.

49.  Sponsor departments should develop clear disciplinary procedures for board members of executive NDPBs and NHS bodies with appropriate penalties for failing to observe codes of conduct.

50.  The role of NDPB and NHS accounting officers should be redefined to emphasise their formal responsibility for all aspects of propriety.

51.  The Audit Commission should be authorised to publish public interest reports on NHS bodies at its own discretion.

52.  The Treasury should review the arrangements for external audit of public bodies, with a view to applying the best practices to all.

53.  Each executive NDPB and NHS body that has not already done so should nominate an official or Board Member entrusted with the duty of investigating staff concerns about propriety raised confidentially. Staff should be able to make complaints without going through the normal management structure, and should be guaranteed anonymity. If they remain unsatisfied, staff should also have a clear route for raising concerns about issues of propriety with the sponsor department.

54.  Executive NDPBs, supported by their sponsor departments, should:
     –  develop their own codes of openness, building on the government code and developing good practice on the lines recommended in this report;
     –  ensure that the public are aware of the provisions of their codes;
     –  sponsor departments should encourage executive bodies to follow best practice and improve consistency between similar bodies by working to bring the standards of all up to those of the best;
     –  the Cabinet Office should produce and periodically update guidance on good practice for openness in executive NDPBs and NHS bodies.

55.  New board members should on appointment make a commitment to undertake induction training which should include awareness of public sector values, and standards of probity and accountability.

# NOTE

1.  http://www.public-standards.gov.uk/

# Appendix 5

# Model terms of reference

The following best-practice terms of reference have been developed by the Institute of Chartered Secretaries and Administrators, whose permission for their publication here is accompanied by a clear disclaimer of liability.[1]

This appendix includes model terms of reference for:

- the audit committee;
- the nomination committee;
- the remuneration committee.

### Terms of Reference – Audit Committee

The Combined Code on Corporate Governance (the Combined Code) states that: 'The board should establish formal and transparent arrangements for considering how they should apply the financial reporting and internal control principles and for maintaining an appropriate relationship with the company's auditors.'[2]

The Combined Code goes on to say that the main role and responsibilities of the Audit Committee should be 'set out in written terms of reference'.[3] Such statements express a clear need for an Audit Committee, the requirement for which is also supported by other influential organisations such the Commonwealth Association for Corporate Governance and the International Corporate Governance Network.

The Guidance on Audit Committees (The Smith Report) recognises that 'Audit committee arrangements need to be proportionate to the task, and will vary according to the size, complexity and risk profile of the company.'[4]

As with most aspects of corporate governance, the above principles make it clear that, not only should companies go through a formal process of considering their internal audit and control procedures and evaluating their relationship with their external auditor, but they must be seen to be doing so in a fair and thorough manner. It is, therefore, essential that the

Audit Committee is properly constituted with a clear remit and identified authority.

As regards the make up of the Committee, we have followed the Combined Code and recommend a minimum of three independent non-executive directors (although two is permissible for smaller companies).[5] The board should satisfy itself that at least one member of the Committee has recent and relevant financial experience. We have made specific recommendations that others may be required to assist the Committee from time to time, according to the particular items being considered and discussed.

Although not a provision in the Code, the Higgs review states as good practice, in its Non-Code Recommendations, that the company secretary (or their designee) should act as secretary to the Committee. The Smith Report states that the company secretary should attend the Audit Committee. It is the company secretary's responsibility to ensure that the board and its Committees are properly constituted and advised. There also needs to be a clear co-ordination between the main board and the various Committees where the company secretary would normally act as a valued intermediary. In addition, although the responsibility for internal controls clearly remains with the board as a whole, the company secretary would normally have the day-to-day task of reviewing the internal control procedures of the company and responsibility for drafting the governance report.

The frequency with which the Committee needs to meet will vary from company to company and may change from time to time. As a general rule, most Audit Committees would be expected to meet quarterly – the Combined Code provides that the Committee should meet at least three times a year.

The list of duties we have proposed are those which we believe all Audit Committees should consider. Some companies may wish to add to this list and some smaller companies may need to modify it in other ways. The Combined Code includes a provision for a report on the Audit Committee to be included in the company's annual report.

Such a report will need to disclose the following:

- role and main responsibilities of the Audit Committee;
- composition of committee, including relevant qualifications and experience; the appointment process; and any fees paid in respect of membership;
- number of meetings and attendance levels;
- a description of the main activities of the year to:
  - monitor the integrity of the financial statements;
  - review the integrity of the internal financial control and risk management systems;

- review the independence of the external auditors, and the provision of non-audit services;
- describe the oversight of the external audit process, and how its effectiveness was assessed;
- explain the recommendation to the board on the appointment of auditors.

There is clearly a need for there to be a guiding document for the effective operation of the Audit Committee. This has led the ICSA to produce this Guidance Note proposing model terms of reference for an Audit Committee.

The document draws on the experience of senior Company Secretaries and best practice as carried out in some of the country's leading companies.

Companies which have a US listing may need to amend these terms in light of the requirements of the recently introduced rules following the Sarbanes–Oxley Act.

The Combined Code also requires that the terms of reference of the Audit Committee, explaining its role and the authority delegated to it by the board, be made available on request and placed on the company's website.[6]

While this Guidance Note is aimed primarily at the corporate sector, the doctrine of good governance, including the introduction of Audit Committees, is increasingly being recognised and adopted by other organisations particularly in the public and not for profit sectors. The principles underlying the content of this Guidance Note are applicable regardless of the size or type of organisation and we trust that it will be useful across all sectors.

**Model Terms of Reference – Audit Committee**
Reference to 'the Committee' shall mean the Audit Committee.
Reference to 'the board' shall mean the board of directors.
The square brackets contain recommendations which are in line with best practice but which may need to be changed to suit the circumstances of the particular organisation.

*1. Membership*
1.1    Members of the Committee shall be appointed by the board, on the recommendation of the Nomination Committee in consultation with the Chairman of the Audit Committee. The Committee shall be made up of at least [3] members.
1.2    All members of the Committee shall be independent non-executive directors at least one of whom shall have recent and relevant financial experience. The Chairman of the board shall not be a member of the Committee.

1.3   Only members of the Committee have the right to attend Committee meetings. However, other individuals such as the Chairman of the board, Chief Executive, Finance Director, other directors, the heads of risk, compliance and internal audit and representatives from the finance function may be invited to attend all or part of any meeting as and when appropriate.

1.4   The external auditors will be invited to attend meetings of the Committee on a regular basis.

1.5   Appointments to the Committee shall be for a period of up to three years, which may be extended for two further three year periods, provided the director remains independent.

1.6   The board shall appoint the Committee Chairman who shall be an independent non-executive director. In the absence of the Committee Chairman and/or an appointed deputy, the remaining members present shall elect one of themselves to chair the meeting.

*2. Secretary*

2.1   The company secretary or their nominee shall act as the secretary of the Committee.

*3. Quorum*

3.1 The quorum necessary for the transaction of business shall be [2] members. A duly convened meeting of the Committee at which a quorum is present shall be competent to exercise all or any of the authorities, powers and discretions vested in or exercisable by the Committee.

*4. Frequency of Meetings*

4.1   The Committee shall meet [at least three times a year at appropriate times in the reporting and audit cycle] [quarterly on the first Wednesday in each of January, April, July and October] and otherwise as required.

*5. Notice of Meetings*

5.1   Meetings of the Committee shall be summoned by the secretary of the Committee at the request of any of its members or at the request of external or internal auditors if they consider it necessary.

5.2   Unless otherwise agreed, notice of each meeting confirming the venue, time and date, together with an agenda of items to be discussed, shall be forwarded to each member of the Committee, any other person required to attend and all other non-executive directors, no later than [5] working days before the date of the meeting. Supporting papers shall be sent to Committee members and to other attendees as appropriate, at the same time.

## 6. Minutes of Meetings

6.1   The secretary shall minute the proceedings and resolutions of all meetings of the Committee, including recording the names of those present and in attendance.

6.2   The secretary shall ascertain, at the beginning of each meeting, the existence of any conflicts of interest and minute them accordingly.

6.3   Minutes of Committee meetings shall be circulated promptly to all members of the Committee and, once agreed, to all members of the board.

## 7. Annual General Meeting

7.1   The Chairman of the Committee shall attend the Annual General Meeting prepared to respond to any shareholder questions on the Committee's activities.

## 8. Duties

The Committee should carry out the duties below for the parent company, major subsidiary undertakings and the group as a whole, as appropriate.

8.1   Financial Reporting

8.1.1   The Committee shall monitor the integrity of the financial statements of the company, including its annual and interim reports, preliminary results' announcements and any other formal announcement relating to its financial performance, reviewing significant financial reporting issues and judgements which they contain. The Committee shall also review summary financial statements, significant financial returns to regulators and any financial information contained in certain other documents, such as announcements of a price sensitive nature.

8.1.2   The Committee shall review and challenge where necessary:

8.1.2.1   the consistency of, and any changes to, accounting policies both on a year on year basis and across the company/group;

8.1.2.2   the methods used to account for significant or unusual transactions where different approaches are possible;

8.1.2.3   whether the company has followed appropriate accounting standards and made appropriate estimates and judgements, taking into account the views of the external auditor;

8.1.2.4   the clarity of disclosure in the company's financial reports and the context in which statements are made; and

8.1.2.5   all material information presented with the financial statements, such as the operating and financial review and the corporate governance statement (insofar as it relates to the audit and risk management);

8.1.3   The Committee shall review the annual financial statements of the pension funds where not reviewed by the board as a whole.

8.2   Internal Controls and Risk Management Systems

The Committee shall:

8.2.1   keep under review the effectiveness of the company's internal controls and risk management systems; and

8.2.2   review and approve the statements to be included in the annual report concerning internal controls and risk management [unless this is done by the board as a whole].

8.3   Whistleblowing

The Committee shall review the company's arrangements for its employees to raise concerns, in confidence, about possible wrongdoing in financial reporting or other matters. The Committee shall ensure that these arrangements allow proportionate and independent investigation of such matters and appropriate follow up action.

8.4   Internal Audit

The Committee shall:

8.4.1   monitor and review the effectiveness of the company's internal audit function in the context of the company's overall risk management system;

8.4.2   approve the appointment and removal of the head of the internal audit function;

8.4.3   consider and approve the remit of the internal audit function and ensure it has adequate resources and appropriate access to information to enable it to perform its function effectively and in accordance with the relevant professional standards. The Committee shall also ensure the function has adequate standing and is free from management or other restrictions;

8.4.4   review and assess the annual internal audit plan;

8.4.5   review promptly all reports on the company from the internal auditors;

8.4.6   review and monitor management's responsiveness to the findings and recommendations of the internal auditor; and

8.4.7   meet the head of internal audit at least once a year, without management being present, to discuss their remit and any issues arising from the internal audits carried out. In addition, the head of internal audit shall be given the right of direct access to the Chairman of the board and to the Committee.

8.5   External Audit

The Committee shall:

8.5.1    consider and make recommendations to the board, to be put to shareholders for approval at the AGM, in relation to the appointment, re-appointment and removal of the company's external auditor. The Committee shall oversee the selection process for new auditors and if an auditor resigns the Committee shall investigate the issues leading to this and decide whether any action is required;

8.5.2    oversee the relationship with the external auditor including (but not limited to):

8.5.2.1    approval of their remuneration, whether fees for audit or non-audit services and that the level of fees is appropriate to enable an adequate audit to be conducted;

8.5.2.2    approval of their terms of engagement, including any engagement letter issued at the start of each audit and the scope of the audit;

8.5.2.3    assessing annually their independence and objectivity taking into account relevant [UK] professional and regulatory requirements and the relationship with the auditor as a whole, including the provision of any non-audit services;

8.5.2.4    satisfying itself that there are no relationships (such as family, employment, investment, financial or business) between the auditor and the company (other than in the ordinary course of business);

8.5.2.5    agreeing with the board a policy on the employment of former employees of the company's auditor, then monitoring the implementation of this policy;

8.5.2.6    monitoring the auditor's compliance with relevant ethical and professional guidance on the rotation of audit partners, the level of fees paid by the company compared to the overall fee income of the firm, office and partner and other related requirements; and

8.5.2.7    assessing annually their qualifications, expertise and resources and the effectiveness of the audit process which shall include a report from the external auditor on their own internal quality procedures;

8.5.3    meet regularly with the external auditor, including once at the planning stage before the audit and once after the audit at the reporting stage. The Committee shall meet the external auditor at least once a year, without management being present, to discuss their remit and any issues arising from the audit;

8.5.4   review and approve the annual audit plan and ensure that it is consistent with the scope of the audit engagement;

8.5.5   review the findings of the audit with the external auditor. This shall include but not be limited to, the following:

8.5.5.1   a discussion of any major issues which arose during the audit,

8.5.5.2   any accounting and audit judgements, and

8.5.5.3   levels of errors identified during the audit.

The Committee shall also review the effectiveness of the audit.

8.5.6   review any representation letter(s) requested by the external auditor before they are signed by management;

8.5.7   review the management letter and management's response to the auditor's findings and recommendations; and

8.5.8   develop and implement a policy on the supply of non-audit services by the external auditor, taking into account any relevant ethical guidance on the matter.

8.6   Reporting Responsibilities

8.6.1   The Committee Chairman shall report formally to the board on its proceedings after each meeting on all matters within its duties and responsibilities.

8.6.2   The Committee shall make whatever recommendations to the board it deems appropriate on any area within its remit where action or improvement is needed.

8.6.3   The Committee shall compile a report to shareholders on its activities to be included in the company's annual report.

8.7   Other Matters

The Committee shall:

8.7.1   have access to sufficient resources in order to carry out its duties, including access to the company secretariat for assistance as required;

8.7.2   be provided with appropriate and timely training, both in the form of an induction programme for new members and on an ongoing basis for all members;

8.7.3   give due consideration to laws and regulations, the provisions of the Combined Code and the requirements of the UK Listing Authority's Listing Rules as appropriate;

8.7.4   be responsible for co-ordination of the internal and external auditors;

8.7.5   oversee any investigation of activities which are within its terms of reference and act as a court of the last resort; and

8.7.6   at least once a year, review its own performance, constitution and terms of reference to ensure it is operating at maximum effectiveness and recommend any changes it considers necessary to the board for approval.

*9. Authority*

The Committee is authorised:

9.1  to seek any information it requires from any employee of the company in order to perform its duties;

9.2  to obtain, at the company's expense, outside legal or other professional advice on any matter within its terms of reference; and

9.3  to call any employee to be questioned at a meeting of the Committee as and when required.

## Terms of Reference – Nomination Committee

The Combined Code on Corporate Governance (the Combined Code) states that: 'There should be a formal, rigorous and transparent procedure for the appointment of new directors to the board.'[7]

It also provides that: 'There should be a nomination committee which should lead the process for board appointments and make recommendations to the board.'[8]

Previous guidance has permitted smaller listed companies to allow the Board to act as a Nomination Committee. This is no longer the case and, although the Higgs Review recognised that it may take time for smaller companies to comply, it states 'there should be no differentiation in the Code's provision for larger and smaller companies'.[9]

The recommendation is that companies should go through a formal process of reviewing the balance and effectiveness of its Board, identifying the skills needed and those individuals who might best provide them. In particular the committee must assess the time commitments of the Board posts and ensure that the individual has sufficient available time to undertake them.

As with most aspects of Corporate Governance, however, the company must be seen to be doing so in a fair and thorough manner. It is, therefore, essential that a Nomination Committee be properly constituted with a clear remit and identified authority.

The Combined Code states that the majority of members of a Nomination Committee should be independent non-executive directors although it gives no guidance on the overall size of the Committee.[10] We have recommended a Committee of three but companies with larger Boards may wish to consider increasing this to four or five.

Although not a provision in the Combined Code, the Higgs review states as good practice, in its Non-Code Recommendations, that the Company Secretary (or their designee) should act as Secretary to the Committee.[11] It is the Company Secretary's responsibility to ensure that the Board and its Committees are properly constituted and advised. There also needs to be a clear co-ordination between the main Board and the various Committees where the Company Secretary would normally act as a valued intermediary.

The frequency with which the Committee needs to meet will vary considerably from company to company and may change from time to time. It is, however, clear that it must meet close to the year-end to consider whether or not directors retiring by rotation or reaching a pre-determined age limit should be put forward for re-appointment at the Annual General Meeting (AGM) and to review the statement in the annual report concerning its activities. We would recommend that it should meet at least twice a year in order to discharge its responsibilities properly.

The list of duties we have proposed are based on those contained in the Summary of the Principal Duties of the Nomination Committee which ICSA drew up for the Higgs Review, which we believe all Nomination Committees should consider. Some companies may wish to add to this list and some smaller companies may need to modify it in other ways. The Chairman of the Committee should attend the AGM prepared to respond to any questions which may be raised by shareholders on matters within the Committee's area of responsibility.[12]

There is clearly a need for a guiding document for the effective operation of the Nomination Committee. This has led the ICSA to produce this Guidance Note proposing model terms of reference for a Nomination Committee. The document draws on the experience of senior Company Secretaries and best practice as carried out in some of the country's leading companies.

The Combined Code also requires that the terms of reference of the Nomination Committee, explaining its role and the authority delegated to it by the Board, be made available on request and placed on the company's website.[13]

Reference to 'the Committee' shall mean the Nomination Committee.

Reference to 'the Board' shall mean the Board of Directors.

The square brackets contain recommendations which are in line with best practice but which may need to be changed to suit the circumstances of the particular organisation.

## 1. Membership

1.1   Members of the Committee shall be appointed by the Board and shall be made up of least [3] members, the majority of whom should be independent non-executive directors.

1.2   Only members of the Committee have the right to attend Committee meetings. However, other individuals such as the Chief Executive, the head of human resources and external advisers may be invited to attend for all or part of any meeting, as and when appropriate.

1.3   Appointments to the Committee shall be for a period of up to three years, which may be extended for two further three-year periods provided that the majority of the Committee members remain independent.

1.4    The Board shall appoint the Committee Chairman who should be either the Chairman of the Board or an independent non-executive director. In the absence of the Committee Chairman and/or an appointed deputy, the remaining members present shall elect one of their number to chair the meeting. The Chairman of the Board shall not chair the Committee when it is dealing with the matter of succession to the chairmanship.

## 2. Secretary

2.1    The Company Secretary or their nominee shall act as the Secretary of the Committee.

## 3. Quorum

3.1    The quorum necessary for the transaction of business shall be [2] both of whom must be independent non-executive directors. A duly convened meeting of the Committee at which a quorum is present shall be competent to exercise all or any of the authorities, powers and discretions vested in or exercisable by the Committee.

## 4. Frequency of Meetings

4.1    The Committee shall meet [at least twice a year][quarterly on the first Wednesday in each of January, April, July and October] and at such other times as the Chairman of the Committee shall require.[14]

## 5. Notice of Meetings

5.1    Meetings of the Committee shall be summoned by the Secretary of the Committee at the request of the Chairman of the Committee.

5.2    Unless otherwise agreed, notice of each meeting confirming the venue, time and date, together with an agenda of items to be discussed, shall be forwarded to each member of the Committee, any other person required to attend and all other non-executive directors, no later than [5] working days before the date of the meeting. Supporting papers shall be sent to Committee members and to other attendees as appropriate, at the same time.

## 6. Minutes of Meetings

6.1    The Secretary shall minute the proceedings and resolutions of all Committee meetings, including the names of those present and in attendance.

6.2    Minutes of Committee meetings shall be circulated promptly to all members of the Committee and the Chairman of the Board and, once agreed, to all other members of the Board, unless a conflict of interest exists.

## 7. Annual General Meeting

7.1   The Chairman of the Committee shall attend the Annual General Meeting prepared to respond to any shareholder questions on the Committee's activities.

## 8. Duties

8.1   The Committee shall:

8.1.1   regularly review the structure, size and composition (including the skills, knowledge and experience) required of the Board compared to its current position and make recommendations to the Board with regard to any changes;

8.1.2   give full consideration to succession planning for directors and other senior executives in the course of its work, taking into account the challenges and opportunities facing the company, and what skills and expertise are therefore needed on the Board in the future;

8.1.3   be responsible for identifying and nominating for the approval of the Board, candidates to fill board vacancies as and when they arise;

8.1.4   before any appointment is made by the Board, evaluate the balance of skills, knowledge and experience on the board, and, in the light of this evaluation prepare a description of the role and capabilities required for a particular appointment. In identifying suitable candidates the Committee shall:

8.1.4.1   use open advertising or the services of external advisers to facilitate the search;

8.1.4.2   consider candidates from a wide range of backgrounds; and

8.1.4.3   consider candidates on merit and against objective criteria, taking care that appointees have enough time available to devote to the position;

8.1.5   keep under review the leadership needs of the organisation, both executive and non-executive, with a view to ensuring the continued ability of the organisation to compete effectively in the marketplace;

8.1.6   keep up to date and fully informed about strategic issues and commercial changes affecting the company and the market in which it operates;

8.1.7   review annually the time required from non-executive directors. Performance evaluation should be used to assess whether the non-executive directors are spending enough time to fulfil their duties; and

8.1.8   ensure that on appointment to the Board, non-executive directors receive a formal letter of appointment setting out clearly what is expected of them in terms of time commitment, committee service and involvement outside board meetings.

8.2   The Committee shall also make recommendations to the Board concerning:

8.2.1   formulating plans for succession for both executive and non-executive directors and in particular for the key roles of Chairman and Chief Executive (but see 8.2.8 below);

8.2.2   suitable candidates for the role of senior independent director;

8.2.3   membership of the Audit and Remuneration Committees, in consultation with the chairmen of those committees;

8.2.4   the re-appointment of any non-executive director at the conclusion of their specified term of office having given due regard to their performance and ability to continue to contribute to the Board in the light of the knowledge, skills and experience required;

8.2.5   the continuation (or not) in service of any director who has reached the age of [70];

8.2.6   the re-election by shareholders of any director under the 'retirement by rotation' provisions in the company's articles of association having due regard to their performance and ability to continue to contribute to the Board in the light of the knowledge, skills and experience required;

8.2.7   any matters relating to the continuation in office of any director at any time including the suspension or termination of service of an executive director as an employee of the company subject to the provisions of the law and their service contract; and

8.2.8   the appointment of any director to executive or other office other than to the positions of Chairman and Chief Executive, the recommendation for which would be considered at a meeting of the full board.

### 9. Reporting Responsibilities

9.1   The Committee Chairman shall report formally to the Board on its proceedings after each meeting on all matters within its duties and responsibilities.

9.2   The Committee shall make whatever recommendations to the Board it deems appropriate on any area within its remit where action or improvement is needed.

9.3   The Committee shall make a statement in the annual report about its activities, the process used to make appointments and explain if external advice or open advertising has not been used.

### 10. Other

10.1   The Committee shall, at least once a year, review its own performance, constitution and terms of reference to ensure it is operating at

maximum effectiveness and recommend any changes it considers
necessary to the Board for approval.

*11. Authority*
11.1   The Committee is authorised to seek any information it requires
from any employee of the company in order to perform its duties.
11.2   The Committee is authorised to obtain, at the company's expense,
outside legal or other professional advice on any matters within its
terms of reference.

**Terms of Reference – Remuneration Committee**
The Combined Code on Corporate Governance (the Combined Code) states
that: 'There should be a formal and transparent procedure for developing
policy on executive remuneration and for fixing the remuneration packages
of individual directors.'[15]

It goes on to state that: 'The Board should establish a remuneration
committee… [which] should make available its terms of reference,
explaining its role and the authority delegated to it by the Board.'[16]

As with most aspects of corporate governance, the above principles
make it clear that, not only should companies go through a formal process
of considering executive remuneration, but they must be seen to be
doing so in a fair and thorough manner. It is, therefore, essential that the
Remuneration Committee is properly constituted with a clear remit and
identified authority.

The Combined Code recommends the Committee be made up of at least
three independent non-executive directors (although two is permissible
for smaller companies[17]).

Although not a provision in the Combined Code, the Higgs Review
states as good practice, in its Non-Code Recommendations, that the
Company Secretary (or their designee) should act as Secretary to the Committee.[18] It is the Company Secretary's responsibility to ensure that the
Board and its Committees are properly constituted and advised. There also
needs to be a clear co-ordination between the main Board and the various
Committees where the Company Secretary would normally act as a valued
intermediary.

The frequency with which the Committee needs to meet will vary from
company to company and may change from time to time. It is, however,
clear that it must meet close to the year end; to review the Remuneration
Report which is required to be prepared under the Directors' Remuneration
Report Regulations 2002 and be submitted to shareholders with or as part
of the company's Annual Report for their approval at the AGM. We would
recommend that the Committee should meet at least twice a year in order
to discharge its responsibilities properly.

The list of duties we have proposed are those contained within the
Summary of Principle Duties of the Remuneration Committee which

ICSA helped compile for the Higgs Review and which are now appended to the Combined Code. Some companies may wish to add to this list and some smaller companies may need to modify it in other ways. The Combined Code also states that the Chairman of the Committee should attend the AGM prepared to respond to any questions that may be raised by shareholders on matters within the Committee's area of responsibility.[19]

There is clearly a need for there to be a guiding document for the effective operation of the Remuneration Committee. This has led the ICSA to produce this Guidance Note proposing model terms of reference for a Remuneration Committee. The document draws on the experience of senior Company Secretaries and best practice as carried out in some of the country's leading companies.

The Combined Code also requires that the terms of reference of the Remuneration Committee, explaining its role and the authority delegated to it by the Board, be made available on request and placed on the company's website.[20]

References to 'the Committee' shall mean the Remuneration Committee.

References to 'the Board' shall mean the Board of Directors.

The square brackets contain recommendations which are in line with best practice but which may need to be changed to suit the circumstances of the particular organisation.

### 1. Membership

1.1 Members of the Committee shall be appointed by the Board, on the recommendation of the Nomination Committee in consultation with the Chairman of the Remuneration Committee. The Committee shall be made up of at least [3] members, all of whom are independent non-executive directors.

1.2 Only members of the Committee have the right to attend Committee meetings. However, other individuals such as the Chief Executive, the head of human resources and external advisers may be invited to attend for all or part of any meeting as and when appropriate.

1.3 Appointments to the Committee shall be for a period of up to three years, which may be extended for two further three-year periods, provided the director remains independent.

1.4 The Board shall appoint the Committee Chairman who shall be an independent non-executive director. In the absence of the Committee Chairman and/or an appointed deputy, the remaining members present shall elect one of themselves to chair the meeting. The Chairman of the Board shall not be Chairman of the Committee.

### 2. Secretary

2.1 The Company Secretary or their nominee shall act as the Secretary of the Committee.

## 3. Quorum

3.1 The quorum necessary for the transaction of business shall be [2]. A duly convened meeting of the Committee at which a quorum is present shall be competent to exercise all or any of the authorities, powers and discretions vested in or exercisable by the Committee.

## 4. Meetings

4.1 The Committee shall meet [at least twice a year][quarterly on the first Wednesday in each of January, April, July and October] and at such other times as the Chairman of the Committee shall require.[21]

## 5. Notice of Meetings

5.1 Meetings of the Committee shall be summoned by the Secretary of the Committee at the request of any of its members.

5.2 Unless otherwise agreed, notice of each meeting confirming the venue, time and date together with an agenda of items to be discussed, shall be forwarded to each member of the Committee, any other person required to attend and all other non-executive directors, no later than [5] working days before the date of the meeting. Supporting papers shall be sent to Committee members and to other attendees as appropriate, at the same time.

## 6. Minutes of Meetings

6.1 The Secretary shall minute the proceedings and resolutions of all Committee meetings, including the names of those present and in attendance.

6.2 Minutes of Committee meetings shall be circulated promptly to all members of the Committee and, once agreed, to all members of the Board, unless a conflict of interest exists.

## 7. Annual General Meeting

7.1 The Chairman of the Committee shall attend the Annual General Meeting prepared to respond to any shareholder questions on the Committee's activities.

## 8. Duties

The Committee shall:

8.1 determine and agree with the Board the framework or broad policy for the remuneration of the company's Chief Executive, Chairman, the executive directors, the company secretary and such other members of the executive management as it is designated to consider.[22] The remuneration of non-executive directors shall be a matter for the Chairman and the executive members of the Board. No director or manager shall be involved in any decisions as to their own remuneration;

8.2    in determining such policy, take into account all factors which it deems necessary. The objective of such policy shall be to ensure that members of the executive management of the company are provided with appropriate incentives to encourage enhanced performance and are, in a fair and responsible manner, rewarded for their individual contributions to the success of the company;

8.3    review the ongoing appropriateness and relevance of the remuneration policy;

8.4    approve the design of, and determine targets for, any performance related pay schemes operated by the company and approve the total annual payments made under such schemes;

8.5    review the design of all share incentive plans for approval by the Board and shareholders. For any such plans, determine each year whether awards will be made, and if so, the overall amount of such awards, the individual awards to executive directors and other senior executives and the performance targets to be used;

8.6    determine the policy for, and scope of, pension arrangements for each executive director and other senior executives;

8.7    ensure that contractual terms on termination, and any payments made, are fair to the individual, and the company, that failure is not rewarded and that the duty to mitigate loss is fully recognised;

8.8    within the terms of the agreed policy and in consultation with the Chairman and/or Chief Executive as appropriate, determine the total individual remuneration package of each executive director and other senior executives including bonuses, incentive payments and share options or other share awards;

8.9    in determining such packages and arrangements, give due regard to any relevant legal requirements, the provisions and recommendations in the Combined Code and the UK Listing Authority's Listing Rules and associated guidance;

8.10    review and note annually the remuneration trends across the company or group;

8.11    oversee any major changes in employee benefits structures throughout the company or group;

8.12    agree the policy for authorising claims for expenses from the Chief Executive and Chairman;[23]

8.13    ensure that all provisions regarding disclosure of remuneration including pensions, as set out in the Directors' Remuneration Report Regulations 2002 and the Combined Code are fulfilled; and

8.14    be exclusively responsible for establishing the selection criteria, selecting, appointing and setting the terms of reference for any remuneration consultants who advise the committee: and to obtain reliable, up-to-date information about remuneration in other companies. The Committee shall have full authority to commission any reports or surveys which it deems necessary to help it fulfil its obligations.

## 9.   *Reporting Responsibilities*

9.1   The Committee Chairman shall report formally to the Board on its proceedings after each meeting on all matters within its duties and responsibilities.

9.2   The Committee shall make whatever recommendations to the Board it deems appropriate on any area within its remit where action or improvement is needed.

9.3   The Committee shall produce an annual report of the company's remuneration policy and practices which will form part of the company's Annual Report and ensure each year that it is put to shareholders for approval at the AGM.

## *10. Other*

10.1   The Committee shall, at least once a year, review its own performance, constitution and terms of reference to ensure it is operating at maximum effectiveness and recommend any changes it considers necessary to the Board for approval.

## *11. Authority*

11.1   The Committee is authorised by the Board to seek any information it requires from any employee of the company in order to perform its duties.

11.2   In connection with its duties the Committee is authorised by the Board to obtain, at the company's expense, any outside legal or other professional advice.

# NOTES

1.   'The information given in this Guidance Note, is provided in good faith with the intention of furthering the understanding of the subject matter. Whilst we believe the information to be accurate at the time of publication, ICSA and its staff cannot however accept any liability for any loss or damage occasioned by any person or organisation acting or refraining from action as a result of any views expressed therein. If the reader has any specific doubts or concerns about the subject matter they are advised to seek legal advice based on the circumstances of their own situation.' © Institute of Chartered Secretaries and Administrators, 16 Park Crescent, London W1B 1AH (tel: 020 7580 4741; fax: 020 7323 1132).

2.   The Combined Code on Corporate Governance, July 2003, C.3.

3.   The Combined Code on Corporate Governance, July 2003, C.3.2.

4.   Audit Committees – Combined Code Guidance, January 2003, 1.4 Note that references are to the original version published in January 2003. A slightly modified version of the Smith Guidance, with a different numbering sequence, was appended to the Combined Code published in July 2003.

5.  A smaller company is defined as one which is below the FTSE 350 throughout the year immediately before the reporting year.
6.  The Combined Code on Corporate Governance, A.4.1.
7.  The Combined Code on Corporate Governance, July 2003, A.4.
8.  The Combined Code on Corporate Governance, July 2003, A.4.1.
9.  *Review of the Role and Effectiveness of Non-Executive Directors*, January 2003, para 16.8.
10. The Combined Code on Corporate Governance, July 2003, A.4.1. The definition of independence is given in Combined Code provision A.3.1.
11. *Review of the Role and Effectiveness of Non-Executive Directors*, para 11.30.
12. The Combined Code on Corporate Governance, July 2003, D.2.3.
13. The Combined Code on Corporate Governance, July 2003, A.4.1.
14. The frequency and timing of meetings will differ according to the needs of the company. Meetings should be organised so that attendance is maximised (for example by timetabling them to coincide with Board meetings).
15. The Combined Code on Corporate Governance, July 2003, B.2.
16. The Combined Code on Corporate Governance, July 2003, B.2.1.
17. A smaller company is defined as one which is below the FTSE 350 throughout the year immediately before the reporting year.
18. *Review of the Role and Effectiveness of Non-Executive Directors*, January 2003, para 11.30.
19. The Combined Code on Corporate Governance, July 2003, D.2.3.
20. The Combined Code on Corporate Governance, July 2003, A.4.1.
21. The frequency and timing of meetings will differ according to the needs of the company. Meetings should be organised so that attendance is maximised (for example by timetabling them to coincide with Board meetings).
22. Some companies require the Remuneration Committee to consider the packages of all executives at or above a specified level, such as those reporting to a main Board Director, while others require the Committee to deal with all packages above a certain figure.
23. It is suggested that the more common arrangement is for the Chairman of the Board to authorise the Chief Executive's expenses and for the Chairman of the Remuneration Committee to authorise the Chairman's claims. An alternative would be for the Committee to authorise the expenses of both.

# Appendix 6

# Directors' Remuneration Report Regulations 2002, Schedule 7A

**Part 1: Introductory**

1. (1) In the directors' remuneration report for a financial year ('the relevant financial year') there shall be shown the information specified in Parts 2 and 3 below.

   (2) Information required to be shown in the report for or in respect of a particular person shall be shown in the report in a manner that links the information to that person identified by name.

**Part 2: Information not subject to audit**

*Consideration by the directors of matters relating to directors' remuneration*

2. (1) If a committee of the company's directors has considered matters relating to the directors' remuneration for the relevant financial year, the directors' remuneration report shall –

   (a) name each director who was a member of the committee at any time when the committee was considering any such matter;

   (b) name any person who provided to the committee advice, or services, that materially assisted the committee in their consideration of any such matter;

   (c) in the case of any person named under paragraph (b), who is not a director of the company, state –

   (i) the nature of any other services that that person has provided to the company during the relevant financial year; and

   (ii) whether that person was appointed by the committee.

   (2) In sub-paragraph (1)(b) 'person' includes (in particular) any director of the company who does not fall within sub-paragraph (1)(a).

*Statement of company's policy on directors' remuneration*

3.  (1)  The directors' remuneration report shall contain a statement of the company's policy on directors' remuneration for the following financial year and for financial years subsequent to that.

(2)  The policy statement shall include –

(a)  for each director, a detailed summary of any performance conditions to which any entitlement of the director –

(i)   to share options, or

(ii)  under a long-term incentive scheme,

is subject;

(b)  an explanation as to why any such performance conditions were chosen;

(c)  a summary of the methods to be used in assessing whether any such performance conditions are met and an explanation as to why those methods were chosen;

(d)  if any such performance condition involves any comparison with factors external to the company –

(i)   a summary of the factors to be used in making each such comparison, and

(ii)  if any of the factors relates to the performance of another company, of two or more other companies or of an index on which the securities of a company or companies are listed, the identity of that company, of each of those companies or of the index;

(e)  a description of, and an explanation for, any significant amendment proposed to be made to the terms and conditions of any entitlement of a director to share options or under a long term incentive scheme; and

(f)  if any entitlement of a director to share options, or under a long-term incentive scheme, is not subject to performance conditions, an explanation as to why that is the case.

(3)  The policy statement shall, in respect of each director's terms and conditions relating to remuneration, explain the relative importance of those elements which are, and those which are not, related to performance.

(4)  The policy statement shall summarise, and explain, the company's policy on –

(a)  the duration of contracts with directors, and

(b)  notice periods, and termination payments, under such contracts.

(5)  In sub-paragraphs (2) and (3), references to a director are to any person who serves as a director of the company at any time in the period beginning with the end of the relevant financial year and ending with the date on which the directors' remuneration report is laid before the company in general meeting.

*Performance graph*

4. (1) The directors' remuneration report shall –

    (a) contain a line graph that shows for each of –

        (i) a holding of shares of that class of the company's equity share capital whose listing, or admission to dealing, has resulted in the company falling within the definition of 'quoted company', and

        (ii) a hypothetical holding of shares made up of shares of the same kinds and number as those by reference to which a broad equity market index is calculated, a line drawn by joining up points plotted to represent, for each of the financial years in the relevant period, the total shareholder return on that holding; and

    (b) state the name of the index selected for the purposes of the graph and set out the reasons for selecting that index.

  (2) For the purposes of sub-paragraphs (1) and (4), 'relevant period' means the five financial years of which the last is the relevant financial year.

  (3) Where the relevant financial year

    (a) is the company's second, third or fourth financial year, sub-paragraph (2) has effect with the substitution of 'two', 'three' or 'four' (as the case may be) for 'five'; and

    (b) is the company's first financial year, 'relevant period', for the purposes of sub-paragraphs (1) and (4), means the relevant financial year.

  (4) For the purposes of sub-paragraph (1), the 'total shareholder return' for a relevant period on a holding of shares must be calculated using a fair method that –

    (a) takes as its starting point the percentage change over the period in the market price of the holding;

    (b) involves making –

        (i) the assumptions specified in sub-paragraph (5) as to reinvestment of income, and

        (ii) the assumption specified in sub-paragraph (7) as to the funding of liabilities; and

    (c) makes provision for any replacement of shares in the holding by shares of a different description;

and the same method must be used for each of the holdings mentioned in sub-paragraph (1).

  (5) The assumptions as to reinvestment of income are –

    (a) that any benefit in the form of shares of the same kind as those in the holding is added to the holding at the time the benefit becomes receivable; and

    (b) that any benefit in cash, and an amount equal to the value of any benefit not in cash and not falling within paragraph (a), is applied at the time the benefit becomes receivable in the purchase at their market price of shares of the same kind as those in the holding and that the shares purchased are added to the holding at that time.

(6)   In sub-paragraph (5) 'benefit' means any benefit (including, in particular, any dividend) receivable in respect of any shares in the holding by the holder from the company of whose share capital the shares form part.

(7)   The assumption as to the funding of liabilities is that, where the holder has a liability to the company of whose capital the shares in the holding form part, shares are sold from the holding –

(a)   immediately before the time by which the liability is due to be satisfied, and

(b)   in such numbers that, at the time of the sale, the market price of the shares sold equals the amount of the liability in respect of the shares in the holding that are not being sold.

(8)   In sub-paragraph (7) 'liability' means a liability arising in respect of any shares in the holding or from the exercise of a right attached to any of those shares.

*Service contracts*

5.   (1)   The directors' remuneration report shall contain, in respect of the contract of service or contract for services of each person who has served as a director of the company at any time during the relevant financial year, the following information:

(a)   the date of the contract, the unexpired term and the details of any notice periods;

(b)   any provision for compensation payable upon early termination of the contract; and

(c)   such details of other provisions in the contract as are necessary to enable members of the company to estimate the liability of the company in the event of early termination of the contract.

(2)   The directors' remuneration report shall contain an explanation for any significant award made to a person in the circumstances described in paragraph 14.

## Part 3: Information subject to audit

*Amount of each director's emoluments and compensation in the relevant financial year*

6.   (1)   The directors' remuneration report shall for the relevant financial year show, for each person who has served as a director of the company at any time during that year, each of the following –

(a)   the total amount of salary and fees paid to or receivable by the person in respect of qualifying services;

(b)   the total amount of bonuses so paid or receivable;

(c) the total amount of sums paid by way of expenses allowance that are –

    (i) chargeable to United Kingdom income tax (or would be if the person were an individual); and

    (ii) paid to or receivable by the person in respect of qualifying services;

(d) the total amount of –

    (i) any compensation for loss of office paid to or receivable by the person, and

    (ii) any other payments paid to or receivable by the person in connection with the termination of qualifying services;

(e) the total estimated value of any benefits received by the person otherwise than in cash that –

    (i) do not fall within any of sub-paragraphs (a) to (d) or paragraphs 7 to 11 below,

    (ii) are emoluments of the person, and

    (iii) are received by the person in respect of qualifying services; and

(f) the amount that is the total of the sums mentioned in paragraphs (a) to (e).

(2) The directors' remuneration report shall show, for each person who has served as a director of the company at any time during the relevant financial year, the amount that for the financial year preceding the relevant financial year is the total of the sums mentioned in paragraphs (a) to (e) of sub-paragraph (1).

(3) The directors' remuneration report shall also state the nature of any element of a remuneration package which is not cash.

(4) The information required by sub-paragraphs (1) and (2) shall be presented in tabular form.

*Share options*

7. (1) The directors' remuneration report shall contain, in respect of each person who has served as a director of the company at any time in the relevant financial year, the information specified in paragraph 8.

(2) Sub-paragraph (1) is subject to paragraph 9 (aggregation of information to avoid excessively lengthy reports).

(3) The information specified in paragraphs (a) to (c) of paragraph 8 shall be presented in tabular form in the report.

(4) In paragraph 8 'share option', in relation to a person, means a share option granted in respect of qualifying services of the person.

8. The information required by sub-paragraph (1) of paragraph 7 in respect of such a person as is mentioned in that sub-paragraph is –

(a) the number of shares that are subject to a share option –

    (i) at the beginning of the relevant financial year or, if later, on the date of the appointment of the person as a director of the company, and

(ii)   at the end of the relevant financial year or, if earlier, on the cessation of the person's appointment as a director of the company, in each case differentiating between share options having different terms and conditions;

(b)   information identifying those share options that have been awarded in the relevant financial year, those that have been exercised in that year, those that in that year have expired unexercised and those whose terms and conditions have been varied in that year;

(c)   for each share option that is unexpired at any time in the relevant financial year –

(i)   the price paid, if any, for its award,

(ii)   the exercise price,

(iii)   the date from which the option may be exercised, and

(iv)   the date on which the option expires;

(d)   a description of any variation made in the relevant financial year in the terms and conditions of a share option;

(e)   a summary of any performance criteria upon which the award or exercise of a share option is conditional, including a description of any variation made in such performance criteria during the relevant financial year;

(f)   for each share option that has been exercised during the relevant financial year, the market price of the shares, in relation to which it is exercised, at the time of exercise; and

(g)   for each share option that is unexpired at the end of the relevant financial year –

(i)   the market price at the end of that year, and

(ii)   the highest and lowest market prices during that year, of each share that is subject to the option.

9.   (1)   If, in the opinion of the directors of the company, disclosure in accordance with paragraphs 7 and 8 would result in a disclosure of excessive length then, (subject to sub-paragraphs (2) and (3)) –

(a)   information disclosed for a person under paragraph 8(a) need not differentiate between share options having different terms and conditions;

(b)   for the purposes of disclosure in respect of a person under paragraph 8(c)(i) and (ii) and (g), share options may be aggregated and (instead of disclosing prices for each share option) disclosure may be made of weighted average prices of aggregations of share options;

(c)   for the purposes of disclosure in respect of a person under paragraph 8(c)(iii) and (iv), share options may be aggregated and (instead of disclosing dates for each share option) disclosure may be made of ranges of dates for aggregation of share options.

(2)   Sub-paragraph (1)(b) and (c) does not permit the aggregation of –

(a)   share options in respect of shares whose market price at the end of the relevant financial year is below the option exercise price, with (b)　share options in respect of shares whose market price at the end of the relevant financial year is equal to, or exceeds, the option exercise price.

(3)　Sub-paragraph (1) does not apply (and accordingly, full disclosure must be made in accordance with paragraphs 7 and 8) in respect of share options that during the relevant financial year have been awarded or exercised or had their terms and conditions varied.

*Long term incentive schemes*

10.　(1)　The directors' remuneration report shall contain, in respect of each person who has served as a director of the company at any time in the relevant financial year, the information specified in paragraph 11.

(2)　Sub-paragraph (1) does not require the report to contain share option details that are contained in the report in compliance with paragraphs 7 to 9.

(3)　The information specified in paragraph 11 shall be presented in tabular form in the report.

(4)　For the purposes of paragraph 11 –

(a)　'scheme interest', in relation to a person, means an interest under a long term incentive scheme that is an interest in respect of which assets may become receivable under the scheme in respect of qualifying services of the person; and

(b)　such an interest 'vests' at the earliest time when –

(i)　it has been ascertained that the qualifying conditions have been fulfilled, and

(ii)　the nature and quantity of the assets receivable under the scheme in respect of the interest have been ascertained.

(5)　In this Schedule 'long term incentive scheme' means any agreement or arrangement under which money or other assets may become receivable by a person and which includes one or more qualifying conditions with respect to service or performance that cannot be fulfilled within a single financial year, and for this purpose the following shall be disregarded, namely –

(a)　any bonus the amount of which falls to be determined by reference to service or performance within a single financial year;

(b)　compensation in respect of loss of office, payments for breach of contract and other termination payments; and

(c)　retirement benefits.

11.　(1)　The information required by sub-paragraph (1) of paragraph 10 in respect of such a person as is mentioned in that sub-paragraph is –

(a)　details of the scheme interests that the person has at the beginning of the relevant financial year or if later on the date of the appointment of the person as a director of the company;

(b)　details of the scheme interests awarded to the person during the relevant financial year;

        (c)   details of the scheme interests that the person has at the end of the relevant financial year or if earlier on the cessation of the person's appointment as a director of the company;

        (d)   for each scheme interest within paragraphs (a) to (c) –

            (i)    the end of the period over which the qualifying conditions for that interest have to be fulfilled (or if there are different periods for different conditions, the end of whichever of those periods ends last); and

            (ii)   a description of any variation made in the terms and conditions of the scheme interests during the relevant financial year; and

        (e)   for each scheme interest that has vested in the relevant financial year –

            (i)    the relevant details (see sub-paragraph (3)) of any shares,

            (ii)   the amount of any money, and

           (iii)  the value of any other assets, that have become receivable in respect of the interest.

    (2)   The details that sub-paragraph (1)(b) requires of a scheme interest awarded during the relevant financial year include, if shares may become receivable in respect of the interest, the following –

        (a)   the number of those shares;

        (b)   the market price of each of those shares when the scheme interest was awarded; and

        (c)   details of qualifying conditions that are conditions with respect to performance.

    (3)   In sub-paragraph (1)(e)(i) 'the relevant details', in relation to any shares that have become receivable in respect of a scheme interest, means –

        (a)   the number of those shares;

        (b)   the date on which the scheme interest was awarded;

        (c)   the market price of each of those shares when the scheme interest was awarded;

        (d)   the market price of each of those shares when the scheme interest vested; and

        (e)   details of qualifying conditions that were conditions with respect to performance.

*Pensions*

12.   (1)   The directors' remuneration report shall, for each person who has served as a director of the company at any time during the relevant financial year, contain the information in respect of pensions that is specified in sub-paragraphs (2) and (3).

    (2)   Where the person has rights under a pension scheme that is a defined benefit scheme in relation to the person and any of those rights are rights to which he has become entitled in respect of qualifying services of his –

    (a)  details

        (i)  of any changes during the relevant financial year in the person's accrued benefits under the scheme, and

        (ii)  of the person's accrued benefits under the scheme as at the end of that year;

    (b)  the transfer value, calculated in a manner consistent with 'Retirement Benefit Schemes – Transfer Values (GN 11)' published by the Institute of Actuaries and the Faculty of Actuaries and dated 6th April 2001, of the person's accrued benefits under the scheme at the end of the relevant financial year;

    (c)  the transfer value of the person's accrued benefits under the scheme that in compliance with paragraph (b) was contained in the directors' remuneration report for the previous financial year or, if there was no such report or no such value was contained in that report, the transfer value, calculated in such a manner as is mentioned in paragraph (b), of the person's accrued benefits under the scheme at the beginning of the relevant financial year;

    (d)  the amount obtained by subtracting –

        (i)  the transfer value of the person's accrued benefits under the scheme that is required to be contained in the report by paragraph (c), from

        (ii)  the transfer value of those benefits that is required to be contained in the report by paragraph (b),

        and then subtracting from the result of that calculation the amount of any contributions made to the scheme by the person in the relevant financial year.

  (3)  Where –

    (a)  the person has rights under a pension scheme that is a money purchase scheme in relation to the person, and

    (b)  any of those rights are rights to which he has become entitled in respect of qualifying services of his, details of any contribution to the scheme in respect of the person that is paid or payable by the company for the relevant financial year or paid by the company in that year for another financial year.

*Excess retirement benefits of directors and past directors*

13.  (1)  Subject to sub-paragraph (3), the directors' remuneration report shall show in respect of each person who has served as a director of the company –

    (a)  at any time during the relevant financial year, or

    (b)  at any time before the beginning of that year, the amount of so much of retirement benefits paid to or receivable by the person under pension schemes as is in excess of the retirement benefits to which he was entitled on the date on which the benefits first became payable or 31st March 1997, whichever is the later.

(2)   In subsection (1) 'retirement benefits' means retirement benefits to which the person became entitled in respect of qualifying services of his.

(3)   Amounts paid or receivable under a pension scheme need not be included in an amount required to be shown under sub-paragraph (1) if –

   (a)   the funding of the scheme was such that the amounts were or, as the case may be, could have been paid without recourse to additional contributions; and

   (b)   amounts were paid to or receivable by all pensioner members of the scheme on the same basis;
        and in this sub-paragraph 'pensioner member', in relation to a pension scheme, means any person who is entitled to the present payment of retirement benefits under the scheme.

(4)   In this paragraph –

   (a)   references to retirement benefits include benefits otherwise than in cash; and

   (b)   in relation to so much of retirement benefits as consists of a benefit otherwise than in cash, references to their amount are to the estimated money value of the benefit;

and the nature of any such benefit shall also be shown in the report.

*Compensation for past directors*

14.   The directors' remuneration report shall contain details of any significant award made in the relevant financial year to any person who was not a director of the company at the time the award was made but had previously been a director of the company, including (in particular) compensation in respect of loss of office and pensions but excluding any sums which have already been shown in the report under paragraph 6(1)(d).

*Sums paid to third parties in respect of a director's services*

15.   (1)   The directors' remuneration report shall show, in respect of each person who served as a director of the company at any time during the relevant financial year, the aggregate amount of any consideration paid to or receivable by third parties for making available the services of the person –

   (a)   as a director of the company, or

   (b)   while director of the company –

      (i)    as director of any of its subsidiary undertakings, or

      (ii)   as director of any other undertaking of which he was (while director of the company) a director by virtue of the company's nomination (direct or indirect), or

      (iii)  otherwise in connection with the management of the affairs of the company or any such other undertaking.

(2)  The reference to consideration includes benefits otherwise than in cash; and in relation to such consideration the reference to its amount is to the estimated money value of the benefit.

The nature of any such consideration shall be shown in the report.

(3)  The reference to third parties is to persons other than –

(a)  the person himself or a person connected with him or a body corporate controlled by him, and

(b)  the company or any such other undertaking as is mentioned in sub-paragraph (1)(b)(ii).

# Appendix 7

# Useful websites

Corporate governance is a hugely topical subject and, therefore, there is a large number of useful websites to which anyone wishing more information can turn. The website associated with this book is www.itgovernance.co.uk/corporate_governance.aspx. In addition to the specific sites mentioned in the text of this book (from which key documents can be downloaded), some of the most useful sites include:

- AuditNet.org: www.auditnet.org/index.htm
- Corporate Governance (US): www.corpgov.net
- The Corporate Library (US): www.thecorporatelibrary.com
- Department of Trade and Industry (UK): www.dti.gov.uk/bbf/corp-govern ance/page15267.html
- Encyclopedia about corporate governance: www.encycogov.com
- European Corporate Governance Institute: www.ecgi.org/index.htm
- Financial Reporting Council (UK): www.frc.org.uk
- Financial Services Authority (UK): www.fsa.gov.uk
- FTSE Corporate Governance Indices (UK): www.ftse.com/Indices/FTSE_ Corporate_Governance_Index_Series/index.jsp
- Governance Publishing (UK): www.governance.co.uk
- ICAEW (UK): www.icaew.com/index.cfm?route=127640
- International Corporate Governance Network: www.icgn.org
- National Association of Corporate Directors (US): www.nacdonline.org
- Office of Government Commerce (UK): www.ogc.gov.uk
- Office of Governmentwide Policy, General Services Administration (US): www.gsa.gov
- Sarbanes–Oxley made understandable: www.sarbanesoxleysimplified.com

# Appendix 8

# Further reading

These books are all available through the accompanying website: www.it governance.co.uk/corporate_governance.aspx.

Bottomley, S (2007) *The Constitutional Corporation: Rethinking corporate governance*, Ashgate Publishing, Aldershot

Calder, A (2005) *IT Governance: Guidelines for directors*, IT Governance Publishing, Ely

Chambers, A (2005) *Tottel's Corporate Governance Handbook*, 3rd edn, Tottel Publishing, Haywards Heath

Chandler, D (2005) *Strategic Corporate Social Responsibility: Stakeholders in a global environment*, Sage Publications, London

Charan, R (2005) *Boards that Deliver: Advancing corporate governance from compliance to competitive advantage*, J Wiley, Chichester

Chew, D H and Gillian, S L (2004) *Corporate Governance at the Crossroads: A book of readings*, McGraw-Hill, Maidenhead

Clarke, T (2004) *Theories of Corporate Governance*, Routledge, London

Colley, J *et al* (2005) *What is Corporate Governance?*, McGraw-Hill, Maidenhead

Dallas, G (2004) *Governance and Risk: An analytical handbook for investors, managers, directors and stakeholders*, McGraw-Hill, Maidenhead

Davies, A (2006) *Best Practice in Corporate Governance: Building reputation and sustainable success*, Gower Publishing, Aldershot

Douglas, L N and Brownsword, R (2006) *Global Governance and the Quest for Justice*, Hart Publishing, Oxford

Eadie, D (2001) *Extraordinary Board Leadership: The seven keys to high-impact governance*, Jones & Bartlett, Sudbury, MA

Euromoney Yearbooks (2007) *International Corporate Governance Review*, 5th edn, Euromoney Yearbooks, Colchester

Gandossy, R and Sonnenfeld, J (2004) *Leadership and Governance from the Inside Out*, J Wiley, Chichester

Gregoriou, G N and Ali, P (2006) *International Corporate Governance after Sarbanes Oxley*, J Wiley, Chichester

Harvard Business School (2000) *Harvard Business Review on Corporate Governance*, Harvard Business School Press, Boston, MA

Keasey, K, Thompson, S and Wright, M (2005) *Corporate Governance: Accountability, enterprise and international comparisons*, J Wiley, Chichester

Light, M (2001) *The Strategic Board: The step-by-step guide to high impact governance*, J Wiley, Chichester

Mallin, C (2004) *Corporate Governance*, Oxford University Press, Oxford

Mallin, C (2006) *Handbook on International Corporate Governance: Country analyses*, Edward Elgar Publishing, Cheltenham

O'Brien, J (2005) *Governing the Corporation*, J Wiley, Chichester

Pierce, C (2004) *Handbook of International Corporate Governance*, Kogan Page, London

Scott, P and Young, D (2004) *Having their Cake...*, Kogan Page, London

Solomon, J (2007) *Corporate Governance and Accountability*, J Wiley, Chichester

Wallace, P and Zinkin, J (2005) *Corporate Governance: Mastering business in Asia*, Ernst & Young LLP, J Wiley, Chichester

Walmsley, K (2005) *Butterworths Corporate Governance Handbook*, LexisNexis Butterworths, London

Wearing, R (2005) *Cases in Corporate Governance*, Sage Publications, London

Young, M R and Nussbaum, K B (2006) *Accounting Regularities and Financial Fraud: A corporate governance guide*, CCH, New York

# Index

# 280   Index